AGES 5-6

LITTLE SKILL SEEKERS
KINDERGARTEN
WORKBOOK

New York • Toronto • London • Auckland • Sydney
Mexico City • New Delhi • Hong Kong • Buenos Aires

Cover Design: Tannaz Fassihi
Cover Illustration: Michael Robertson
Interior Design: Mina Chen; Production: Radames Espinoza
Interior Illustration: Doug Jones

Scholastic Inc., 557 Broadway, New York, NY 10012
ISBN: 978-1-338-60243-2
Copyright © Scholastic Inc.
Published by Scholastic Inc. All rights reserved.
Printed in the U.S.A.
First printing, August 2019.

4 5 6 7 8 9 10   02   25 24 23 22 21 20

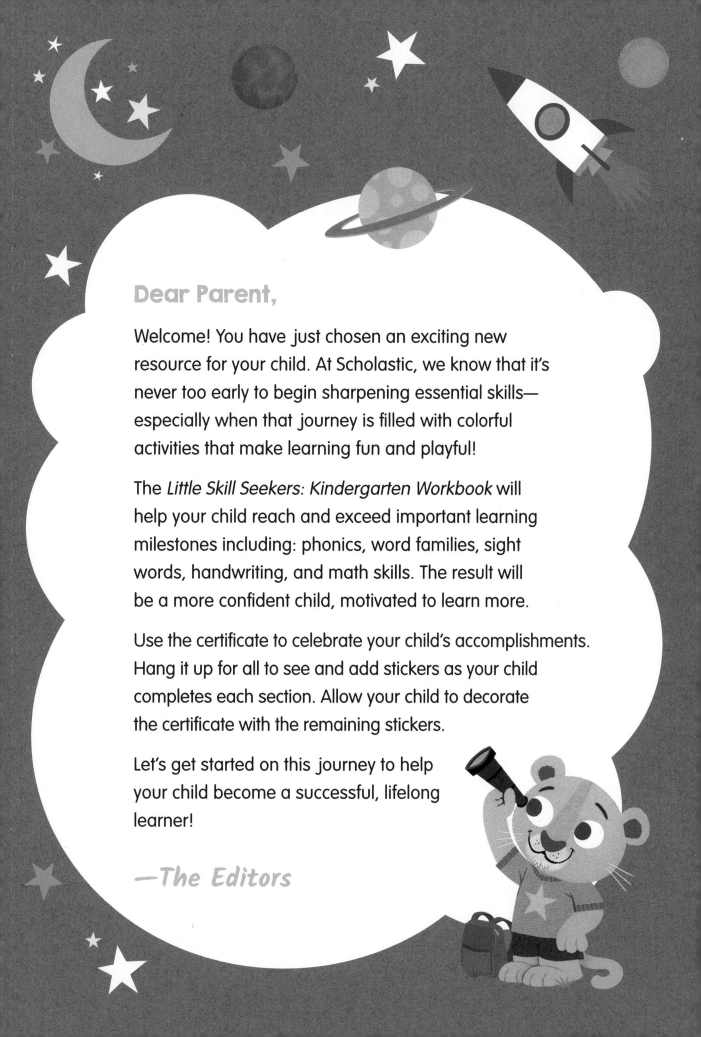

Dear Parent,

Welcome! You have just chosen an exciting new resource for your child. At Scholastic, we know that it's never too early to begin sharpening essential skills—especially when that journey is filled with colorful activities that make learning fun and playful!

The *Little Skill Seekers: Kindergarten Workbook* will help your child reach and exceed important learning milestones including: phonics, word families, sight words, handwriting, and math skills. The result will be a more confident child, motivated to learn more.

Use the certificate to celebrate your child's accomplishments. Hang it up for all to see and add stickers as your child completes each section. Allow your child to decorate the certificate with the remaining stickers.

Let's get started on this journey to help your child become a successful, lifelong learner!

—The Editors

CONTENTS

PHONICS

Cat and hat make the short-*a* sound.
Trace the letter that makes the short-*a* sound in each word.

c a t

h a t

Circle each picture that makes the short-*a* sound.

bag

fan

bib

hen

can

man

Use the picture clues to unscramble each short-*a* word. Write the word on the line.

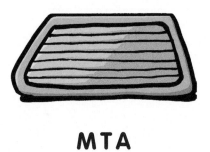

MTA

PAM

_____

AMJ

MPAL

_____

NVA

ANP

_____

Jet and **bed** make the short-*e* sound.
Trace the letter that makes the short-*e* sound in each word.

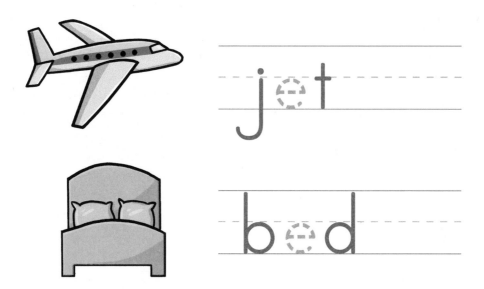

j e t

b e d

Circle each picture that makes the short-e sound.

bug

sled

hen

leg

vest

pin

Label each picture. Use a word from the word bank. Then, circle each picture that makes the short-*e* sound.

Word Bank
nest   deer   tent   vest   shell   tree

_____

_____

_____

_____

_____

_____

Pig and **wig** make the short-*i* sound.
Trace the letter that makes the **short-*i*** sound in each word.

Circle each picture that makes the **short-*i*** sound.

king

gift

car

pin

rip

ten

Use the picture clues to unscramble each short-*i* word. Write the word on the line.

BBI

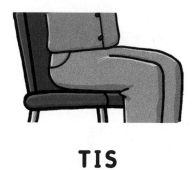

TIS

SHFI

_____

NGIS

_____

ISX

_____

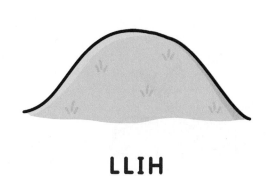

LLIH

_____

Dog and **top** make the short-*o* sound.
Trace the letter that makes the **short-*o*** sound in each word.

dog

top

Circle each picture that makes the short-*o* sound.

net

box

fox

log

chip

frog

Label each picture. Use a word from the word bank. Then, circle each picture that makes the short-*o* sound.

Word Bank					
mop	pot	goat	sock	doll	rose

_____

_____

_____

_____

_____

_____

Rug and **cup** make the short-*u* sound.
Trace the letter that makes the **short-*u*** sound in each word.

rug

cup

Circle each picture that makes the short-*u* sound.

sun

pig

box

plug

run

duck

Use the picture clues to unscramble each short-*u* word. Write the word on the line.

SBU

_____

MGU

_____

GUB

_____

JGU

_____

UDMR

_____

SKKNU

_____

Name each picture. Which short vowel will finish the word?
Match a short vowel to each picture box.
Then, write the short vowel to finish the word.

h __ m

b __ ll

r __ ng

t __ p

b __ g

e

a

o

u

i

Add a short vowel to each puzzle to make two words. Use the picture clues.

```
        p
    d       g
        t
```

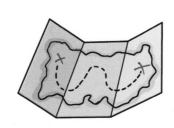

```
        m
    c       t
        p
```

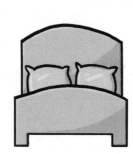

```
        b
    w       b
        d
```

```
        p
    b       b
        g
```

```
        j
    c       p
        g
```

Snake and **paint** make the long-*a* sound.
Trace the letters that make the long-*a* sound in each word.

snake

paint

Circle each picture that makes the long-*a* sound.

cake

nail

mice

train

crow

tape

Label each picture. Use a word from the word bank.
Then, circle each picture that makes the long-*a* sound.

Word Bank					
cat	lake	rain	bat	eight	hay

_____

_____

_____

Tree and **leaf** make the long-*e* sound.
Trace the letters that make the long-*e* sound in each word.

tree

leaf

Circle each picture that makes the long-*e* sound.

doll

feet

ice

beet

sleep

bee

Use the picture clues to unscramble each long-*e* word. Write the word on the line.

ASEL

NQEEU

ESHEP

SPEA

TTHEE

CEHESE

Kite and **tie** make the long-*i* sound.
Trace the letters that make the **long-*i*** sound in each word.

kite

tie

Circle each picture that makes the **long-*i*** sound.

bike

tire

nine

ice

mask

pig

Label each picture. Use a word from the word bank. Then, circle each picture that makes the long-*i* sound.

Word Bank					
fire	tie	sheep	bike	five	feet

_____

_____

_____

Rose and boat make the long-*o* sound.
Trace the letters that make the long-*o* sound in each word.

rose

boat

Circle each picture that makes the long-*o* sound.

road   plane   goat

fox   bowl   rope

© Scholastic Inc.

Use the picture clues to unscramble each long-o word. Write the word on the line.

OATC

_____

PAOS

_____

OBW

_____

WSNO

_____

EONB

_____

SEON

_____

Mule and fruit make the long-*u* sound.
Trace the letters that make the long-*u* sound in each word.

mule

fruit

Circle each picture that makes the long-*u* sound.

cube   wave   flute

tube   cup   juice

Label each picture. Use a word from the word bank.
Then, circle each picture that makes the long-*u* sound.

Word Bank					
moon	glue	boat	broom	dune	tub

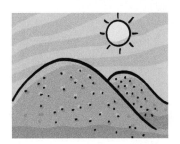

_____

_____

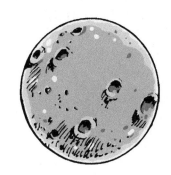

_____

_____

_____

_____

Name each picture. Which letter will finish each long-vowel word? Match a letter to each picture box. Then, write the letter to finish the word.

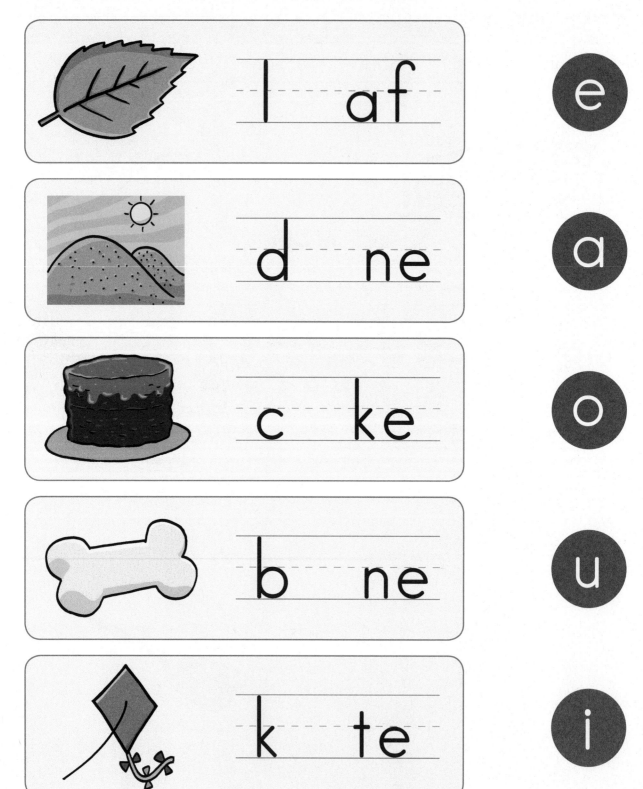

l __ af

e

d __ ne

a

c __ ke

o

b __ ne

u

k __ te

i

Little Skill Seekers

WORD
FAMILIES

-am

Write -am to finish each word.

c|_____   h_____

j_____   y_____

Make more -am words. Use the word wheel.
Write the words. We did the first one for you.

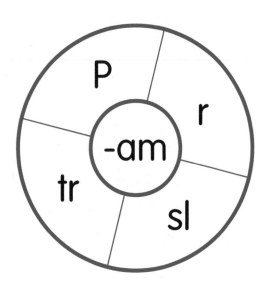

1. ___ram_____

2. _____

3. _____

4. _____

Write -an to finish each word.

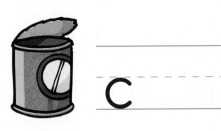 c _____

 m _____

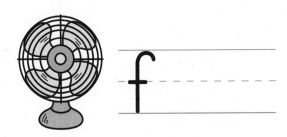 f _____

 v _____

Make more -an words. Use the word wheel.
Write the words. We did the first one for you.

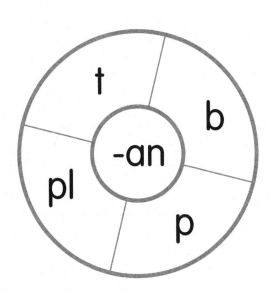

1. _____ ban _____

2. _____

3. _____

4. _____

Write -ap to finish each word.

c|

c ___

m ___

zzzzz

n ___

Make more -ap words. Use the word wheel.
Write the words. We did the first one for you.

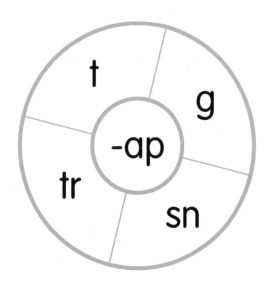

1. ___ gap ___

2. ___

3. ___

4. ___

-at

Write -at to finish each word.

 b _____

 c _____

 h _____

 r _____

Make more -at words. Use the word wheel.
Write the words. The first one is done for you.

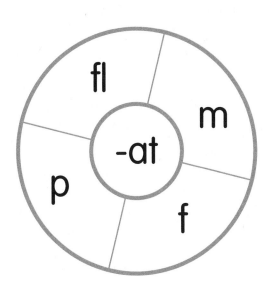

1. _____ mat _____

2. _____

3. _____

4. _____

33

Use the Letter Bank to complete the words in each row.

Letter Bank			
h r tr	_____am	_____am	_____am
c r v	_____an	_____an	_____an
m c fl	_____ap	_____ap	_____ap
b r s	_____at	_____at	_____at

© Scholastic Inc.

Sort the words below into word families.
Write each word in the chart where it belongs.

swam   ran   snap

fan   pat   am

pan   dam   yam

sap   chat

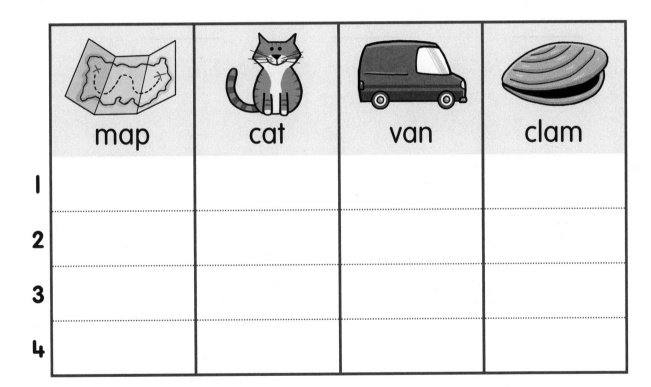

map	cat	van	clam
1			
2			
3			
4			

How many of each did you find? Write the number below.

-ap _____   -at _____   -an _____   -am _____

Which word family has the most words? _____

Add the letters in each box to make words in that word family. Write each word.

-am
h + am = _____
cl + am = _____

-ap
m + ap = _____
n + ap = _____

Use an -am or -ap word from above to finish each sentence. The first one is done for you.

Dan took a ___nap___ on the sofa.

Kam found a _____ in the sand.

Pam loves _____ and eggs.

Bob used a _____ on his trip.

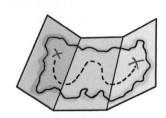

Add the letters in each box to make words in that word family. Write each word.

-an	-at
f + an = _____	c + at = _____
v + an = _____	h + at = _____

Use an -an or -at word from above to finish each sentence. The first one is done for you.

The ___van___ is blue.

The _____ is gray and white.

She wears a pink _____.

I have a _____ in my room.

Write **-ell** to finish each word.

b _____   w _____

sh _____   y _____

Make more **-ell** words. Use the word wheel.
Write the words. The first one is done for you.

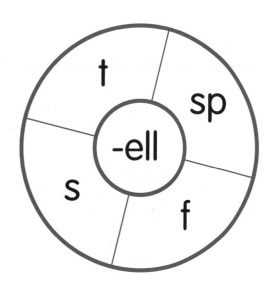

1. _____ spell _____

2. _____

3. _____

4. _____

Write -ick to finish each word.

br _____

s _____

ch _____

st _____

Make more -ick words. Use the word wheel.
Write the words. The first one is done for you.

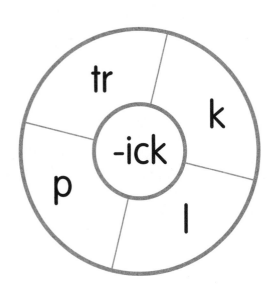

tr

k

-ick

p

l

1. _____kick_____

2. _____

3. _____

4. _____

Write -ill to finish each word.

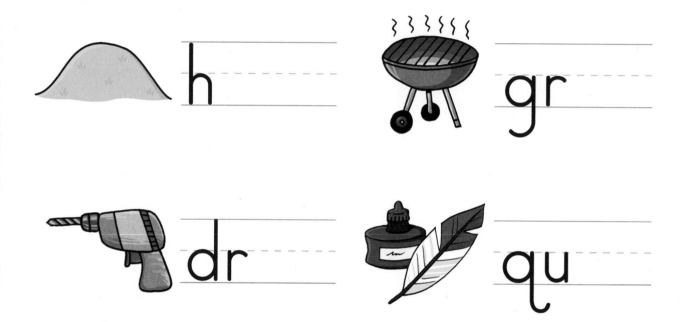

h _____

gr _____

dr _____

qu _____

Make more -ill words. Use the word wheel.
Write the words. The first one is done for you.

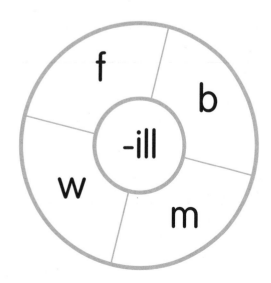

1. _____ bill _____

2. _____

3. _____

4. _____

Write -ing to finish each word.

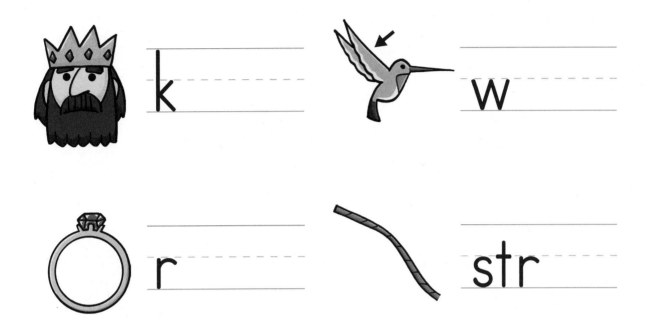

k _____

w _____

r _____

str _____

Make more -ing words. Use the word wheel.
Write the words. The first one is done for you.

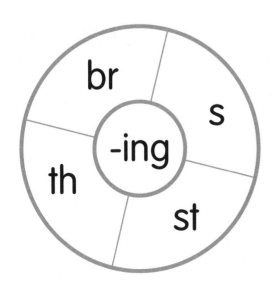

1. ____sing____

2. _____

3. _____

4. _____

Use the Letter Bank to complete the words in each row.

Letter Bank			
sm **sh** **y**	 _____ell	 _____ell	 _____ell
br **s** **st**	 _____ick	 _____ick	 _____ick
gr **b** **sp**	 _____ill	 _____ill	 _____ill
w **sw** **k**	 _____ing	 _____ing	 _____ing

Sort the words below into word families.
Write each word in the chart where it belongs.

ring thick sill spring

brick cell quick well

pick will sing chill wing

chick	shell	quill	king
1			
2			
3			
4			

How many of each did you find? Write the number below.

-ick _____   -ell _____   -ill _____   -ing _____

Which word family has the fewest words? _____

Add the letters in each box to make words in that word family. Write each word.

-ell
sh + ell = _____
b + ell = _____

-ick
k + ick = _____
st + ick = _____

Use an -ell or -ick word from above to finish each sentence. The first one is done for you.

The lunch ____bell____ rings at noon.

The dog brings the _____ back to me.

Dee found a pretty _____ on the shore.

Don't _____ the door.

44

Add the letters in each box to make words from that word family. Write each word.

-ill	-ing
gr + ill = _____	k + ing = _____
h + ill = _____	s + ing = _____

Use an -ill or -ing word from above to finish each sentence. The first one is done for you.

The house is just over that ____hill____.

My parents love to _____ in the summer.

The _____ lives in the castle.

Marci loves to _____.

Write -ip to finish each word.

 dr _____

 s _____

 sh _____

 tr _____

Make more -ip words. Use the word wheel.
Write the words. The first one is done for you.

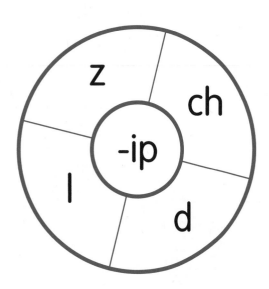

1. _____ chip _____

2. _____

3. _____

4. _____

Write -ock to finish each word.

 b|_____

 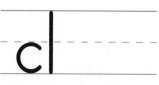 c|_____

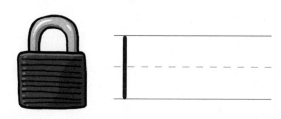 |_____

s_____

Make more -ock words. Use the word wheel.
Write the words. The first one is done for you.

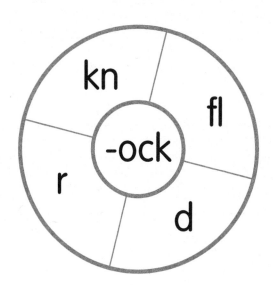

1. _____flock_____

2. _____

3. _____

4. _____

Write -op to finish each word.

m _____

st _____

t _____

p _____

Make more -op words. Use the word wheel.
Write the words. The first one is done for you.

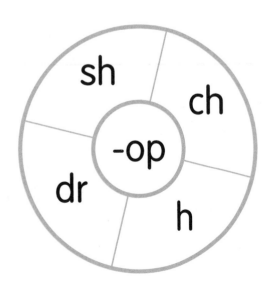

1. _____ chop _____

2. _____

3. _____

4. _____

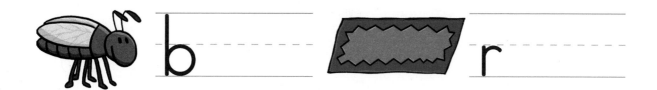

Write -ug to finish each word.

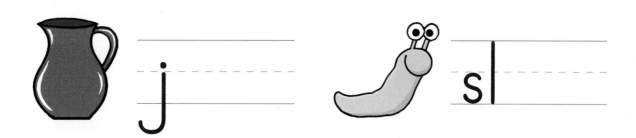

b _____   r _____

j _____   s| _____

Make more -ug words. Use the word wheel.
Write the words. The first one is done for you.

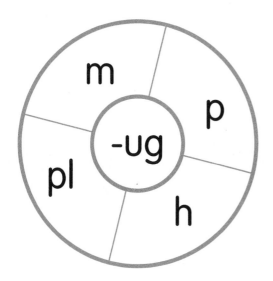

1. _____ pug _____

2. _____

3. _____

4. _____

Use the Letter Bank to complete the words in each row.

Letter Bank			
sh s ch	_____ip	_____ip	_____ip
d r cl	_____ock	_____ock	_____ock
h st m	_____op	_____op	_____op
b m pl	_____ug	_____ug	_____ug

Sort the words below into word families.
Write each word in the chart where it belongs.

tip   knock   tug   drop

flop   zip   plug   mug

hug   lip   top   lock

ship	clock	stop	slug
1			
2			
3			
4			

How many of each did you find? Write the number below.

-ip _____   -ock _____   -op _____   -ug _____

Which two word families have the same number of words?

_____ and _____

Add the letters in each box to make words in that word family. Write each word.

-ip
sh + ip = _____
h + ip = _____

-ock
r + ock = _____
cl + ock = _____

Use an -ip or -ock word from above to finish each sentence. The first one is done for you.

Billy hurt his ___hip___ playing hockey.

Zane sat on a _____.

The cruise _____ left this morning.

We need to repair the _____.

© Scholastic Inc.

Add the letters in each box to make words in that word family. Write each word.

-op
m + op = _____
ch + op = _____

-ug
r + ug = _____
m + ug = _____

Use an -op or -ug word from above to finish each sentence. The first one is done for you.

We need a new ____rug____.

Let's _____ the floor.

This is my favorite _____.

Let's watch Dad _____ wood for the fire.

Write -ail to finish each word.

m _____   p _____

qu _____   sn _____

**Make more -ail words. Use the word wheel.
Write the words. The first one is done for you.**

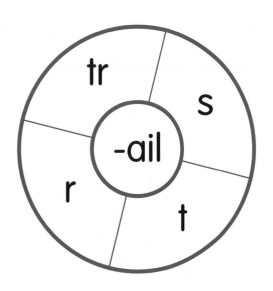

1. _____ sail _____

2. _____

3. _____

4. _____

Write -ake to finish each word.

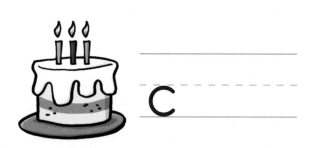 c

 r

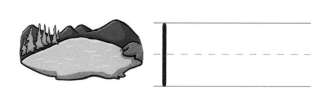 l

 sn

Make more -ake words. Use the word wheel.
Write the words. The first one is done for you.

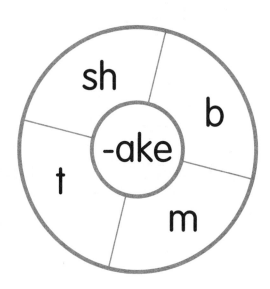

1. __bake__

2. _____

3. _____

4. _____

Write -ay to finish each word.

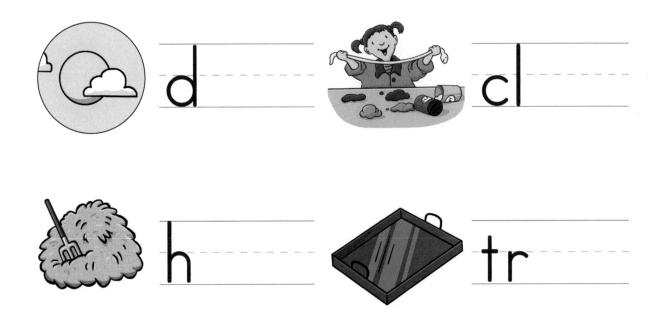

d _____ cl _____

h _____ tr _____

Make more -ay words. Use the word wheel.
Write the words. The first one is done for you.

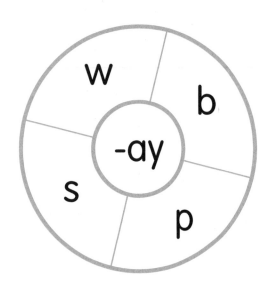

1. ____ bay ____

2. _____

3. _____

4. _____

Write -ee to finish each word.

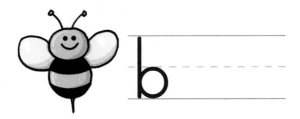

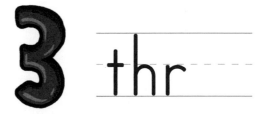

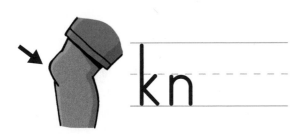

Make more -ee words. Use the word wheel.
Write the words. The first one is done for you.

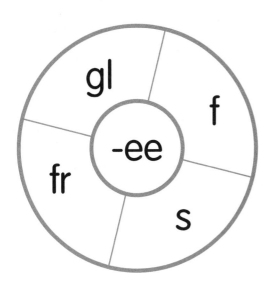

1. _____ fee _____

2. _____

3. _____

4. _____

Use the Letter Bank to complete the words in each row.

Letter Bank			
n s t	_____ail	_____ail	_____ail
w c r	_____ake	_____ake	_____ake
cl tr r d	_____ay	_____ay	_____ay
b tr thr	_____ee	_____ee	_____ee

Sort the words below into word families.
Write each word in the chart where it belongs.

quake   gray   three   pail

sail   shake   tree

glee   stay   tail   trail

quail	cake	hay	bee
1			
2			
3			
4			

How many of each did you find? Write the number below.

| -ail ____ | -ake ____ | -ay ____ | -ee ____ |

Which word family has the most words? _____

Add the letters in each box to make words in that word family. Write each word.

-ail
p + ail = _____
sn + ail = _____

-ake
c + ake = _____
l + ake = _____

Use an -ail or -ake word from above to finish each sentence. The first one is done for you.

I saw a ___snail___ on the grass.

The _____ is frozen.

This _____ is good.

Noah has a red _____.

Add the letters in each box to make words in that word family. Write each word.

-ay
tr + ay = _____
h + ay = _____

-ee
tr + ee = _____
b + ee = _____

Use an -ay or -ee word from above to finish each sentence. The first one is done for you.

He was stung by a ___bee___.

Set the _____ on the table.

She likes to sit under the _____.

Horses eat _____.

Write -eep to finish each word.

sh ____

sw ____

sl ____

st ____

Make more -eep words. Use the word wheel.
Write the words. The first one is done for you.

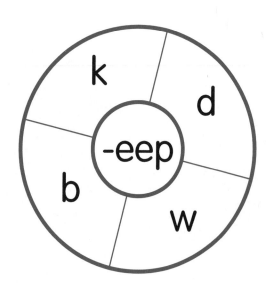

1. ___deep___

2. _____

3. _____

4. _____

Write -ice to finish each word.

 d _____

 sl _____

 m _____

 r _____

Make more -ice words. Use the word wheel.
Write the words. The first one is done for you.

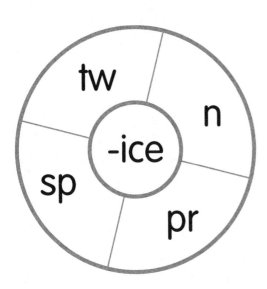

1. _____nice_____

2. _____

3. _____

4. _____

Write -ight to finish each word.

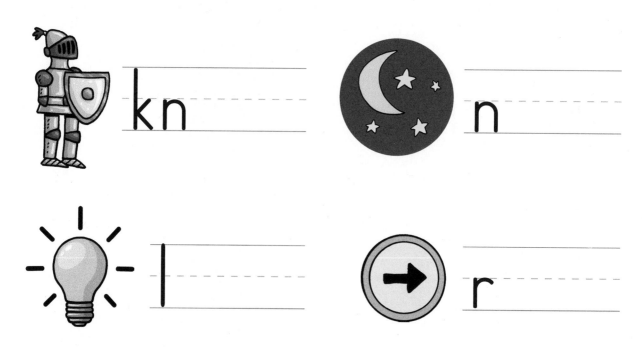

kn _____

n _____

l _____

r _____

Make more -ight words. Use the word wheel.
Write the words. The first one is done for you.

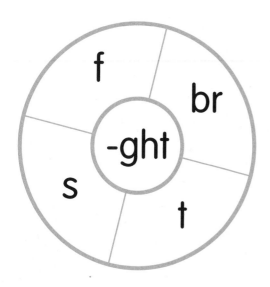

1. ___bright___

2. _____

3. _____

4. _____

Write -ow to finish each word.

 b _____

 sn _____

 cr _____

 bl _____

Make more -ow words. Use the word wheel.
Write the words. The first one is done for you.

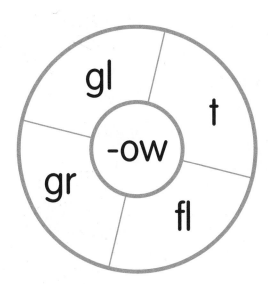

1. _____ tow _____

2. _____

3. _____

4. _____

Use the Letter Bank to complete the words in each row.

Letter Bank			
st sw sh	_____eep	_____eep	_____eep
m sl r	_____ice	_____ice	_____ice
l r n	_____ight	_____ight	_____ight
b cr thr	_____ow	_____ow	_____ow

Sort the words below into word families.
Write each word in the chart where it belongs.

bright   price   grow   beep

deep   glow   mice   low

spice   tight   flow   keep

sheep	dice	right	bow

1
2
3
4

How many of each did you find? Write the number below.

-eep ___   -ice ___   -ight ___   -ow ___

Which word family has the fewest words? _____

Add the letters in each box to make words in that word family. Write each word.

-eep	-ice
sh + eep = _____	d + ice = _____
sl + eep = _____	r + ice = _____

Use an -eep or -ice word from above to finish each sentence. The first one is done for you.

Look at the pretty __sheep__.

We need to _____ soon.

Roll the _____.

Jenny likes _____.

Add the letters in each box to make words in that word family. Write each word.

-ight	-ow
l + ight = _____	sn + ow = _____
n + ight = _____	cr + ow = _____

Use an -ight or -ow word from above to finish each sentence. The first one is done for you.

The __light__ is very bright.

Stars come out at _____.

The _____ flew away.

Kate loves the _____.

Name each picture. Write the word.
Draw a line to match it to the correct word family.

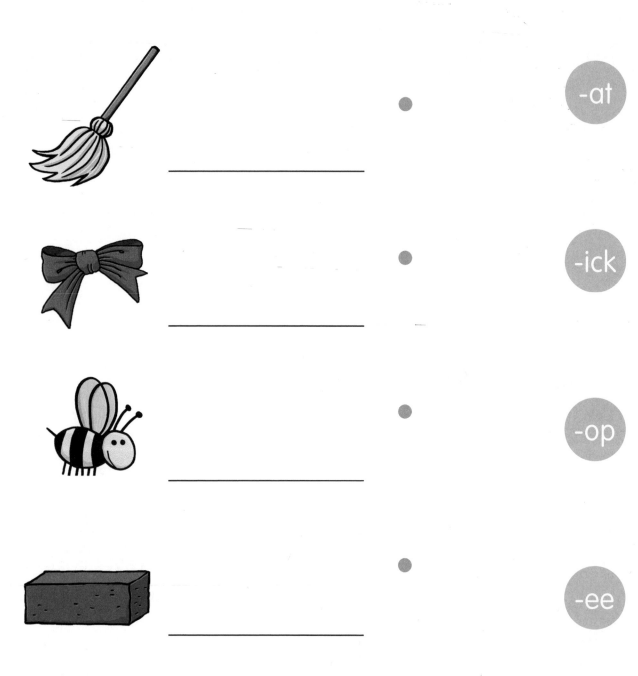

-at

-ick

-op

-ee

-ow

Name each picture. Write the word.
Draw a line to match it to the correct word family.

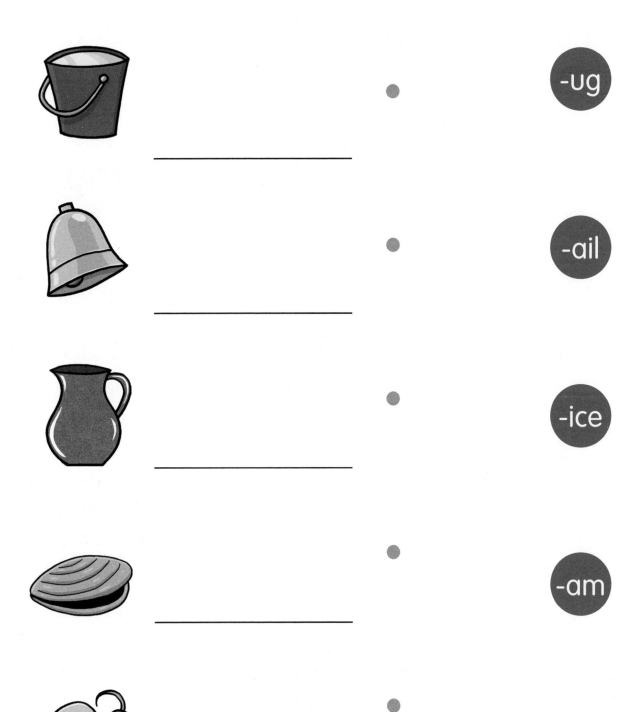

-ug

_____

-ail

_____

-ice

_____

-am

_____

-ell

_____

Label each picture. Use the Word Box.
Match the pictures that are in the same word family.

Word Box					
clay	king	sheep	sweep	tray	ring

Label each picture. Use the Word Box.
Match the pictures that are in the same word family.

Word Box					
clap	clock	lock	map	ship	trip

Color the picture. Use the color key.

If the space has a word from this word family	-an	-ill	-ake	-eep	-ight
Color the space	blue	red	yellow	green	purple

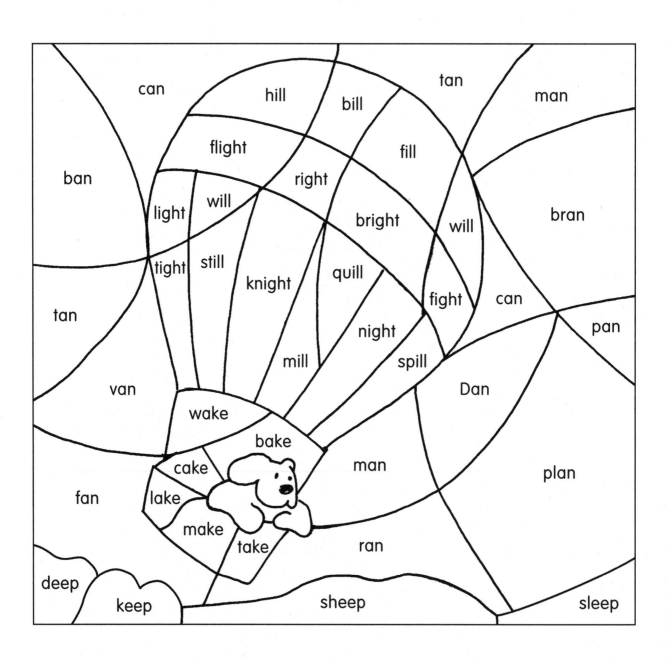

74

Little Skill Seekers

SIGHT WORDS

Trace it.

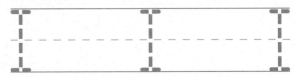

Write it.

Write it.

Write a on each shell.

Color each apple that has I.

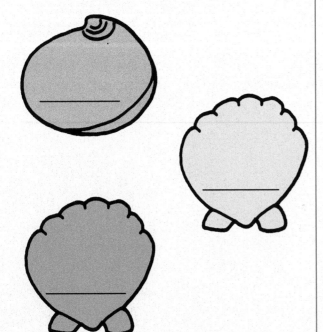

Trace it.

Write it.

Circle each frame that has is.

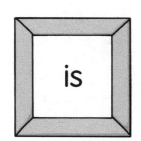
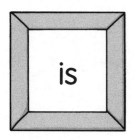
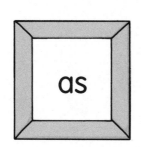

Color each space that has to.

Trace it.

Write it.

Color the letters that spell in.

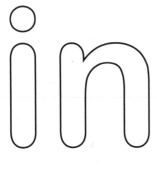

Trace it.

Write it.

Circle each bee with on.

 on

 an

 in

 on

 on

Trace it.

Write it.

Write it on each spaceship.

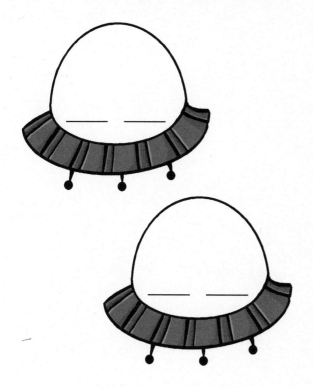

Trace it.

Write it.

Circle each pair of glasses that spell as.

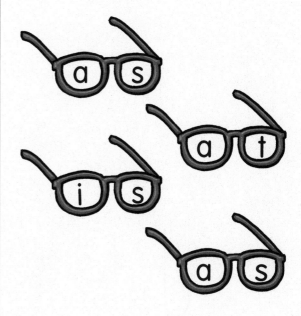

Build a word pyramid. Fill in the letters one at a time.
The first one is done for you.

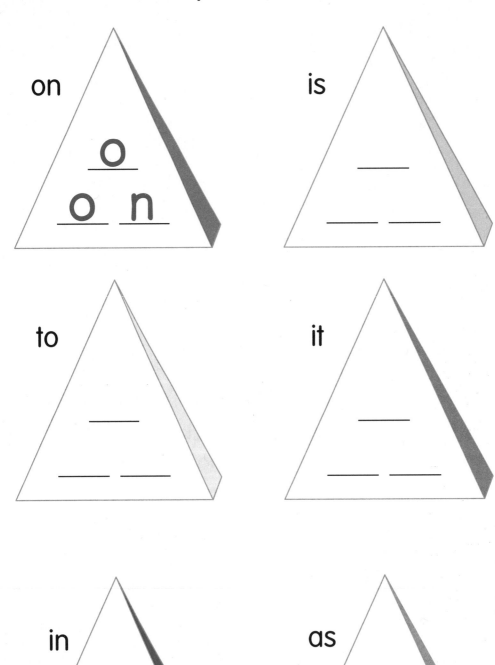

on

$\underline{o}$
$\underline{o}$ $\underline{n}$

is

___

___ ___

to

___

___ ___

it

___

___ ___

in

___

___ ___

as

___

___ ___

Color the picture. Use the color key.

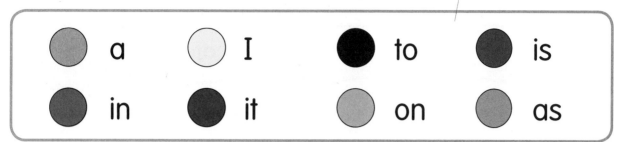

- ● a
- ○ I
- ● to
- ● is
- ● in
- ● it
- ● on
- ● as

Unscramble each sight word.

as   in   to   it   is   on

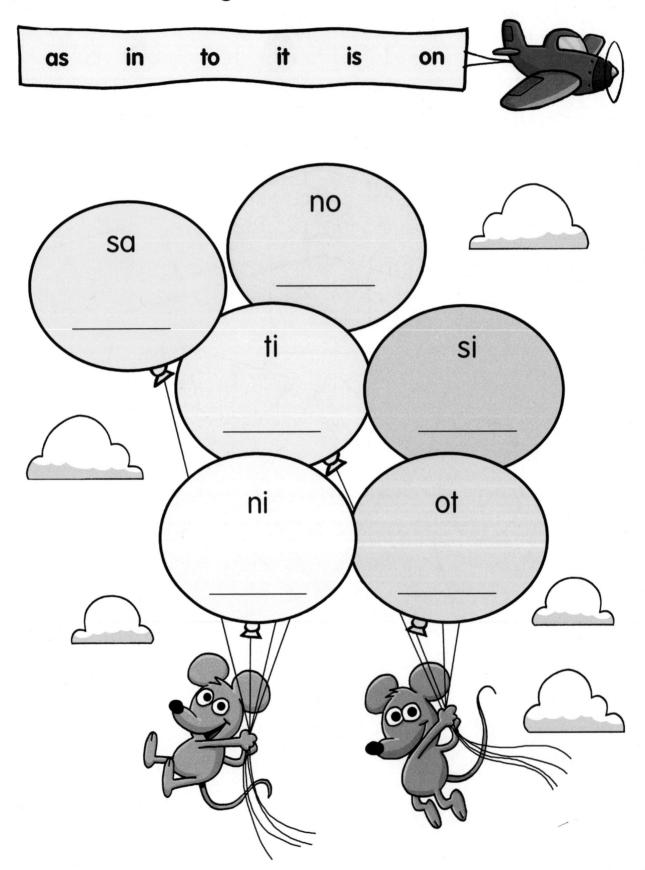

Choose a word from the list to complete the sentences.

Sight Words

| a | as | I | in | is | it | on | to |

1. This _____ my sister Molly.

REMEMBER TO capitalize the first word in a sentence.

2. I have _____ brother too. His name is Paul.

3. Paul and _____ like to swim.

4. Today is as sunny _____ yesterday.

5. _____ is a good day for the beach.

6. We go _____ the beach on sunny days.

7. Molly, what is _____ your beach bag?

8. Paul, put _____ your swim suit.

Trace it.

at at at

be be be

Write it.

Write it.

Color each space with at.

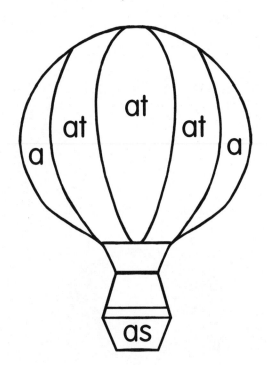

at

at

at

a

a

as

Circle each be.

ba   be

be   he   bu

eb

ve   be

be

Trace it.

Trace it.

an an an

Write it.

Write it.

Write or on each bat.

Trace the path that has an.

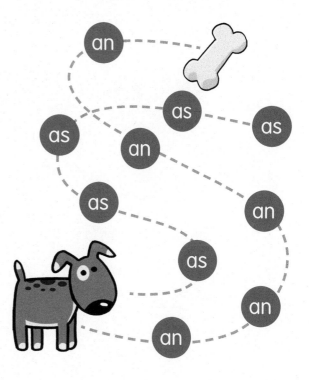

Trace it.

by by by

Trace it.

he he he

Write it.

Write it.

Color the boxes that have by.

by		by
bat		boo
by	be	boy	by
boy	by	by	be

Write he on each ball.

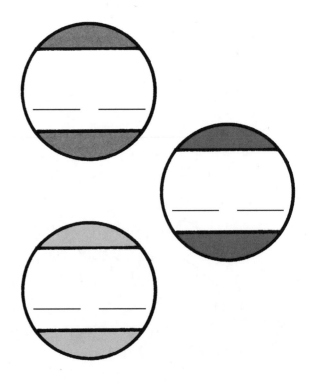

86

Trace it.

Trace it.

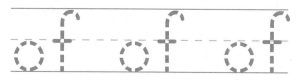

Write it.

- - - - - - - - - - - - -

Write it.

- - - - - - - - - - - - -

Color each hat that has we.

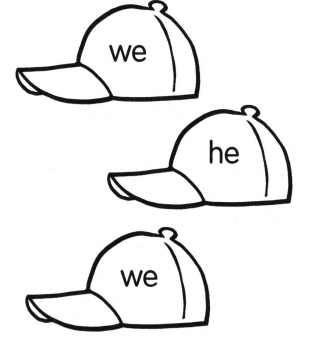

we

he

we

Circle each ice cream scoop that has of.

if

of

of

for

**Build a word pyramid. Fill in the letters one at a time.
The first one is done for you.**

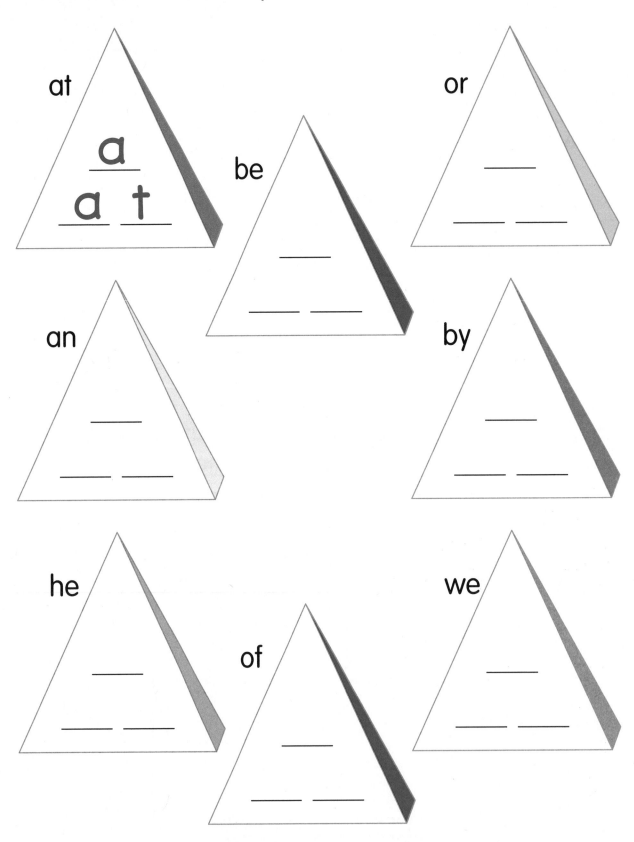

at

a
a t

be

or

an

by

he

of

we

Color the picture. Use the color key.

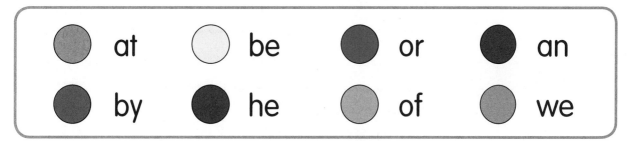

at be or an

by he of we

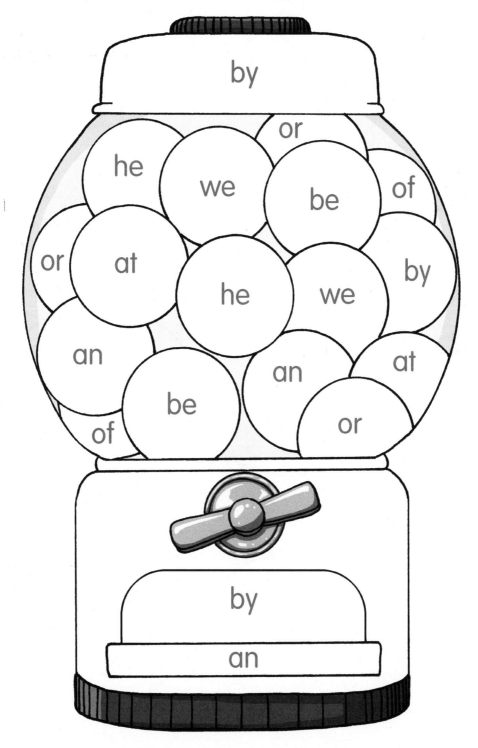

Unscramble each sight word.

at be or an by he we of

ro

na

eb

_____

fo

ew

ta

_____

_____

yb

eh

_____

_____

_____

_____

_____

Choose a word from the list to complete the sentences.

Sight Words

| an | at | be | by | he | of | or | we |

1. I have a twin brother. _____ are in the first grade.

2. We go to school _____ bus.

 REMEMBER TO capitalize the first word in a sentence.

3. Mom always says, "Don't _____ late."

4. The bus comes _____ 8:00 A.M.

5. We must leave early _____ we will miss it.

6. This is a picture _____ George.

7. _____ is the school bus driver.

8. George does _____ important job.

all

and

Trace it.

Trace it.

Write it.

Write it.

Color the letters that spell all.

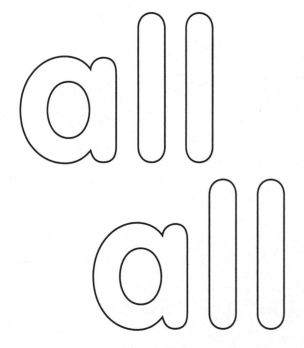

Connect the dots to spell and.

•a

•n

•b

•d

•m

•p

Trace it.

the the

are are

Write it.

Write it.

Write the missing letters to spell the.

Color each balloon that has are.

t ___ e

___ h ___

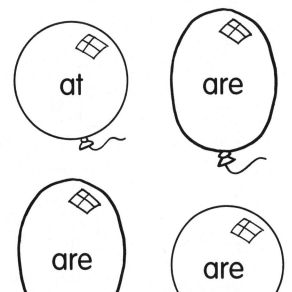

at

are

are

are

Trace it.

Trace it.

Write it.

Write it.

Write for on each bowl.

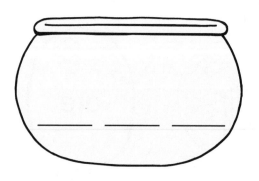

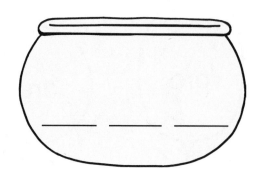

Trace the path that has had.

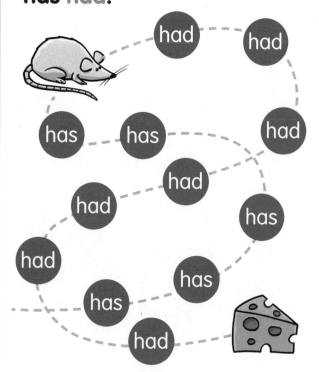

Trace it.

Trace it.

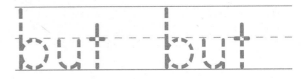

Write it.

Write it.

Color each butterfly wing that has can.

Circle each but.

**Build a word pyramid. Fill in the letters one at a time.
The first one is done for you.**

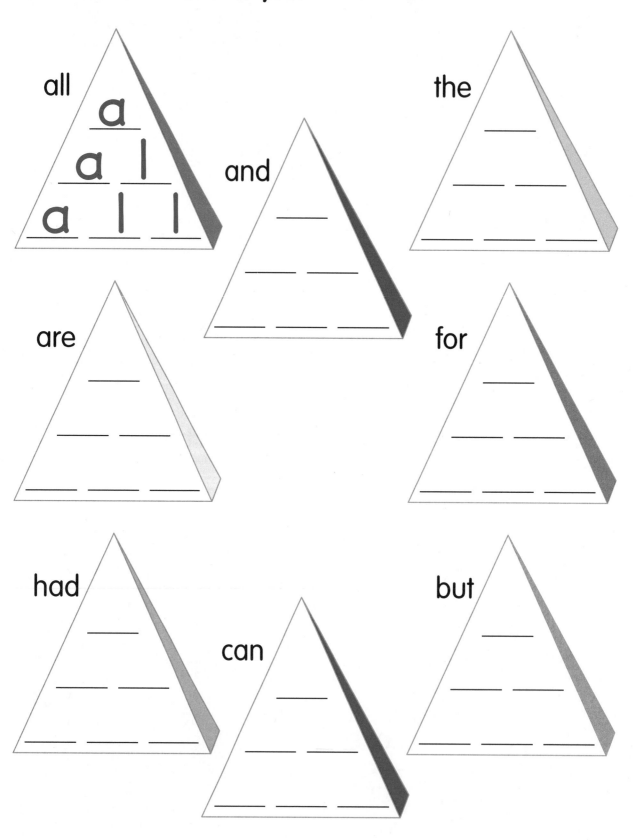

all

the

and

are

for

had

can

but

Color the picture. Use the color key.

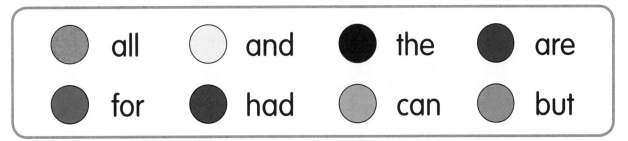

● all   ○ and   ● the   ● are

● for   ● had   ● can   ● but

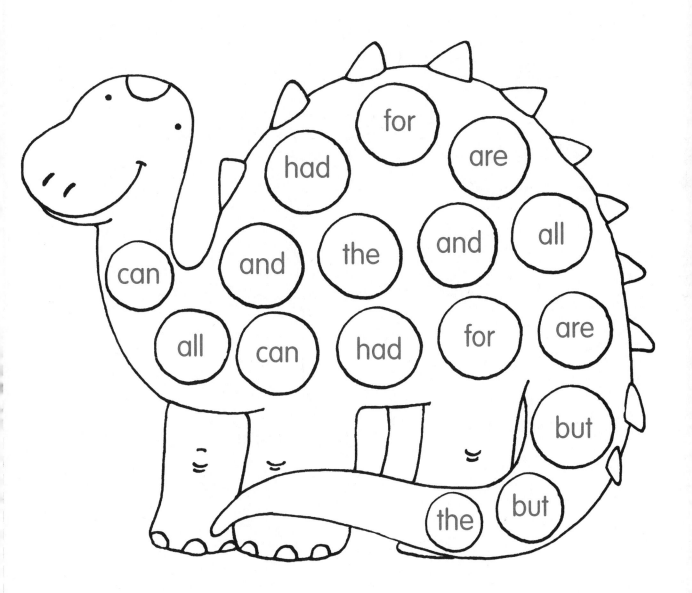

Unscramble each sight word.

all   and   the   are   for   had   can   but

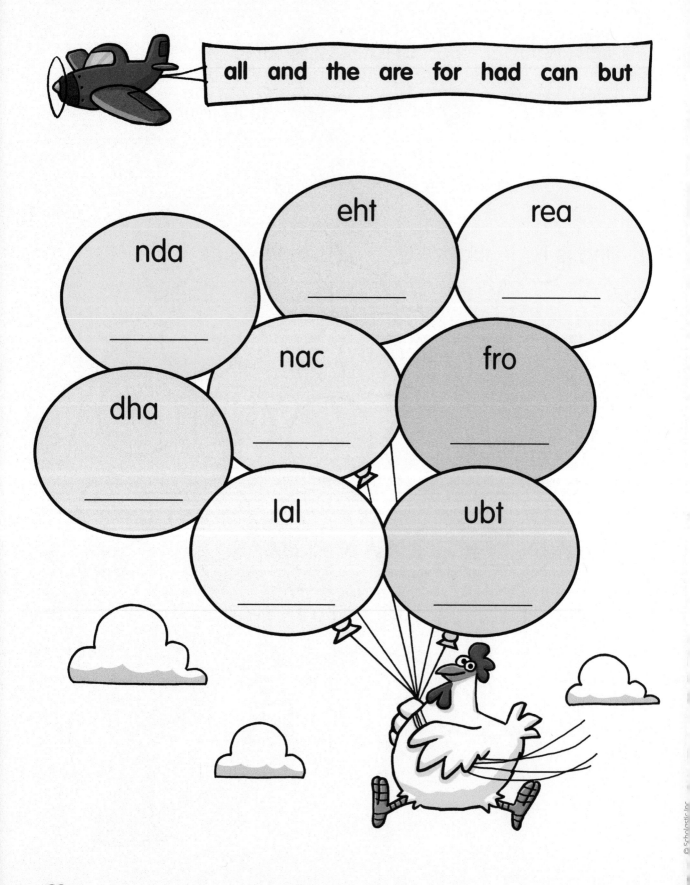

nda

_____

eht

_____

rea

_____

nac

_____

fro

_____

dha

_____

lal

_____

ubt

_____

Choose a word from the list to complete the sentences.

Sight Words

all   and   are   but   can   for   had   the

1. My sisters are _____ older.

2. Lina is 11, Jenna is 13, _____ Ria is 15.

3. Ria is older, _____ Jenna is taller.

4. Jenna and Lina _____ in middle school.

5. They take _____ bus to school.

6. Lina ran _____ class president.

7. She _____ the most votes.

8. I _____ be class president too one day.

Trace it.

Write it.

Trace it.

Write it.

Color each space with you.

you			you
		one	two
yes	you	you	you
you	your	yet	out

Write not on each flag.

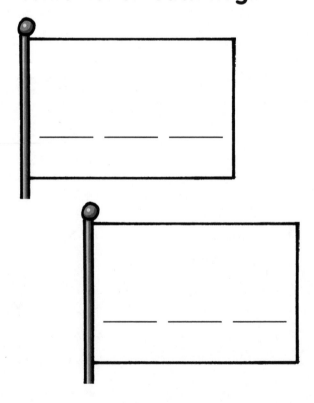

one

Trace it.

one one

Write it.

Circle each one.

one   now

   an   one

one   won

   ran   one

this

Trace it.

this this

Write it.

Color the two socks with the letters that spell this.

th   is   en

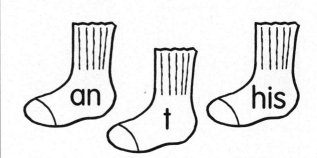

an   t   his

Trace it.

Trace it.

Write it.

Write it.

Write the missing letters to spell from.

Find the word with five times.

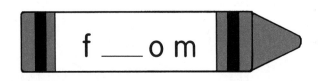

f ___ o m

W	I	T	H	Z	A
I	Q	W	I	T	H
T	I	N	W	S	W
H	N	D	I	B	I
D	X	W	T	X	T
J	E	Z	H	H	H

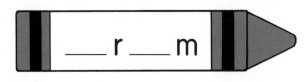

___ r ___ m

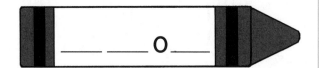

___ ___ o ___

they

Trace it.

they

Write it.

what

Trace it.

what

Write it.

Circle each they.

they

thei

thay

they

they

they

thay

Color each bone that has what.

what

when

where

what

Write each sight word in the shape box it fits. The first one is done for you.

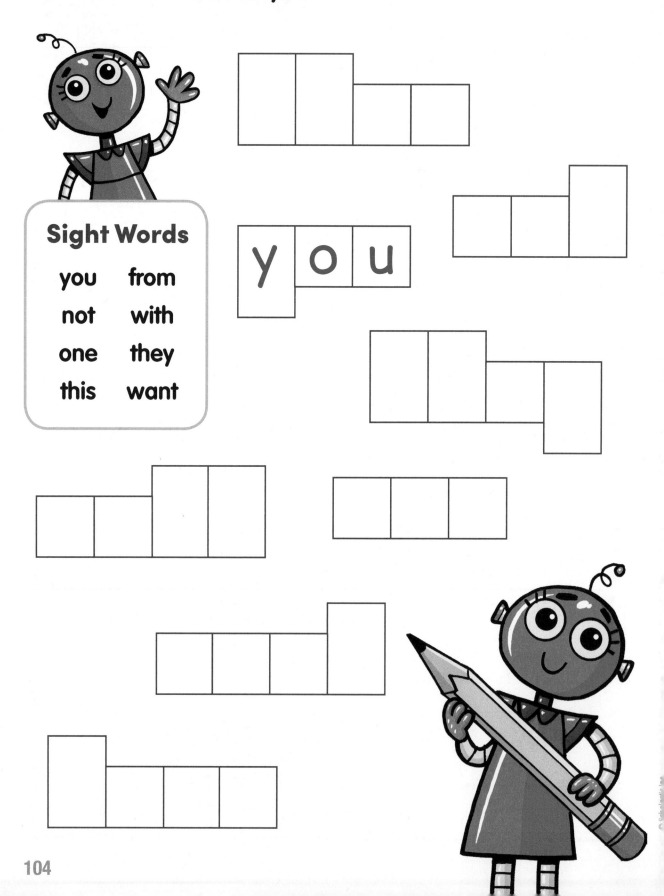

Sight Words

you	from
not	with
one	they
this	want

you

Color the picture. Use the color key.

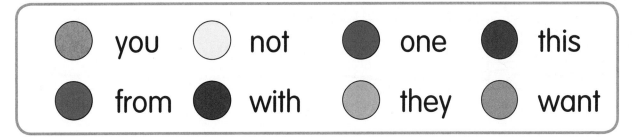

you — not — one — this

from — with — they — want

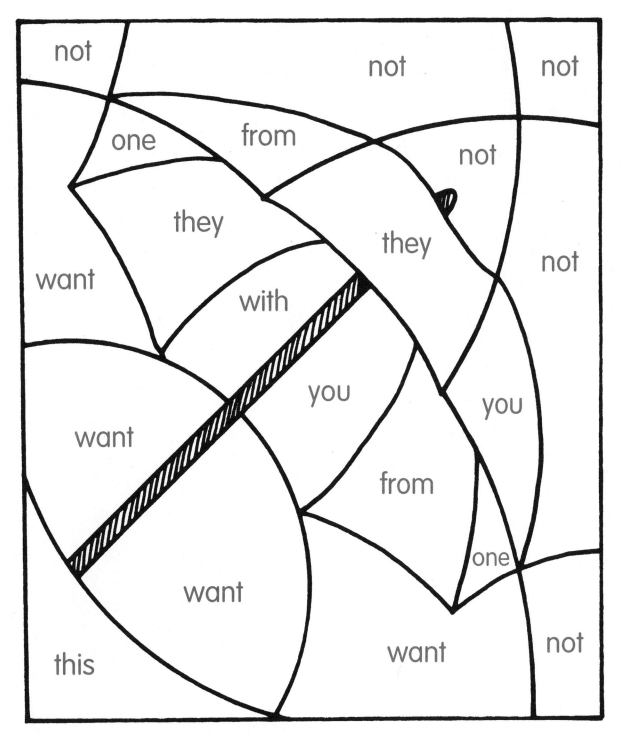

Unscramble each sight word.

you   not   one   this   from   with   they   want

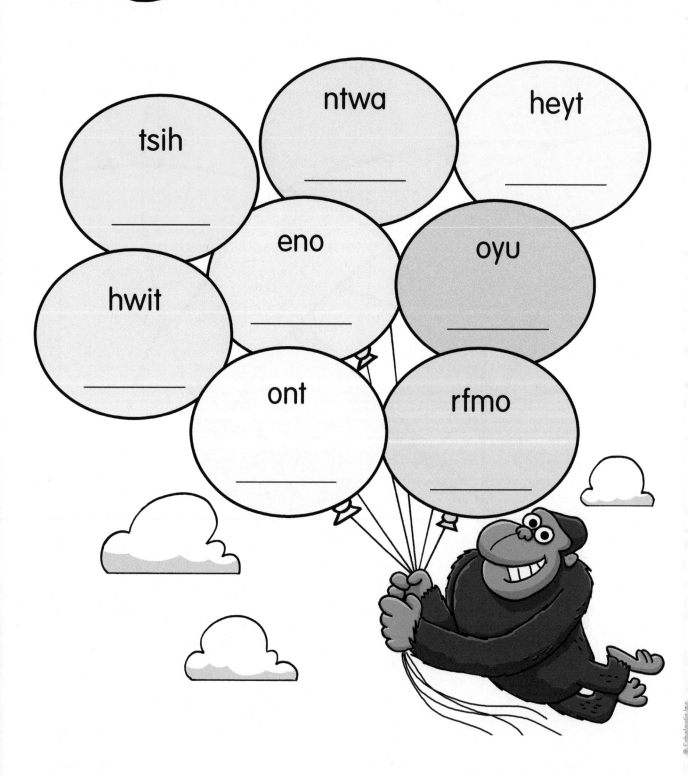

tsih

ntwa
_____

heyt
_____

eno
_____

oyu
_____

hwit
_____

ont
_____

rfmo
_____

Choose a word from the list to complete the sentences.

Sight Words								
from	not	one	they	this	want	with	you	

1. Maya's family is _____ Utah.

REMEMBER TO capitalize the first word in a sentence.

2. _____ moved here last year.

3. _____ is their house.

4. Maya's Grandma lives _____ them.

5. Maya is _____ of my best friends.

6. Maya and I _____ to travel.

7. We do _____ know where yet.

8. _____ can come too!

Trace it.

was   was

she   she

Write it.

Write it.

Connect the dots to spell was.

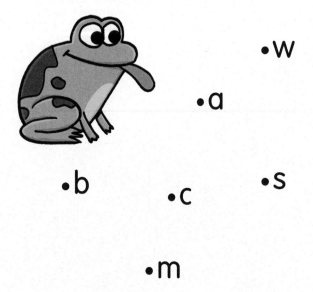

•w

•a

•b   •s

•c

•a   •m

•n

Write she.

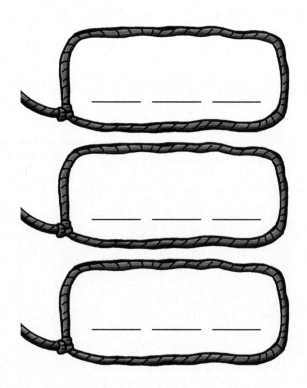

said

were

Trace it.

said

Trace it.

were

Write it.

Write it.

Find the word said five times.

S	A	I	D	Z	A
I	Q	S	A	I	D
S	I	N	S	T	W
A	N	S	A	I	D
I	X	Y	I	A	T
D	E	Z	D	H	H

Color each bubble that has were.

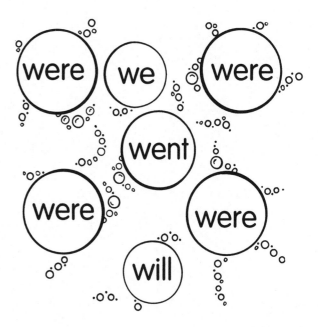

Trace it.

Trace it.

have

Write it.

Write it.

Color each fish that has your.

your

you

pour

your

Circle each have.

have

has

how

have

him

have

Trace it.

when

Trace it.

that

Write it.

Write it.

Color the letters that spell when.

Write the missing letters to spell that.

when
when

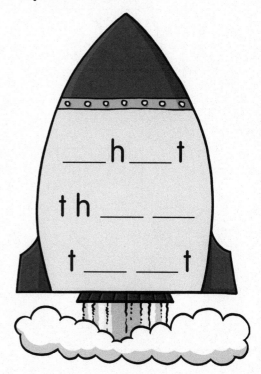

__ h __ t

t h __ __ __

t __ __ t

Write each sight word in the shape box it fits.
The first one is done for you.

Sight Words

was	have
said	were
she	when
that	your

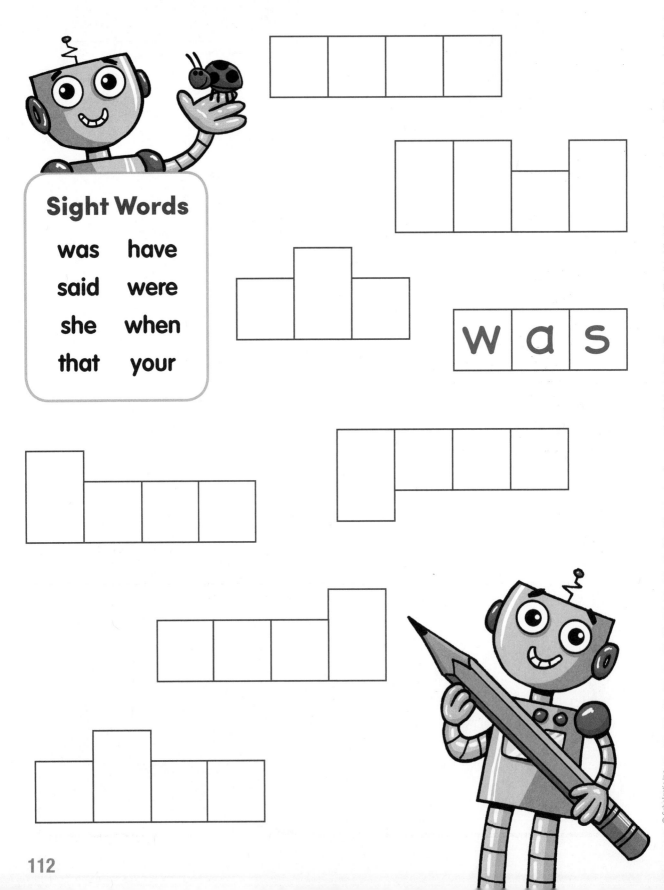

w a s

Color the picture. Use the color key.

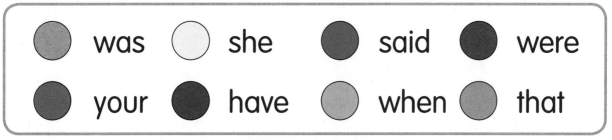

was · she · said · were
your · have · when · that

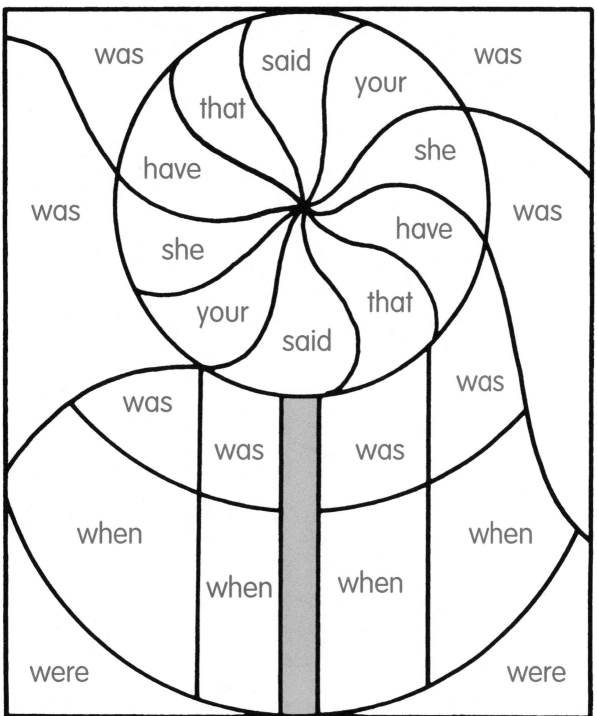

Unscramble each sight word.

| was | she | said | were | your | have | when | that |

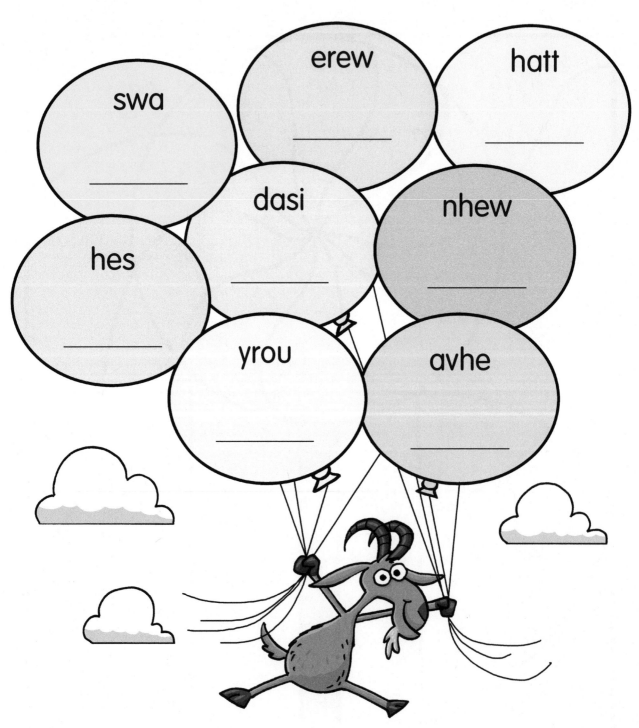

swa

_____

erew

_____

hatt

_____

dasi

_____

nhew

_____

hes

_____

yrou

_____

avhe

_____

Choose a word from the list to complete the sentences.

Sight Words							
have	said	she	that	was	were	when	your

1. Yesterday _____ the first day of school.

2. Ms. Pat will be our new teacher.

_____ teaches first grade.

3. She _____ she loves teaching.

4. What is _____ name?

5. _____ did you start school?

6. _____ you in Kindergarten last year?

7. We will _____ a holiday party this year.

8. I know _____ you will love our class.

Complete the sentences. Choose a word from the list. Write the words in the puzzle. The first one is done for you.

Sight Words

that

the

they

was

what

with

Across

2. Where are _they_ going?

3. I walk to school _____ friends.

4. He _____ at camp all summer.

	¹		

²t h e y

Down

1. Where is _____ dog?

2. Is _____ a new car?

3. _____ is your name?

Read each sentence. Match each sentence with a picture.

●   ● He plays soccer.

●   ● All the mice ate cheese.

●   ● The cats are sleeping.

●   ● They were playing with blocks.

●   ● Mia eats an ice cream cone.

Write a sentence using at least one of the words in blue.

_____

_____

_____

Some words on the board are missing letters. Use the Letter Bank. Fill in the missing letters. The first one is done for you.

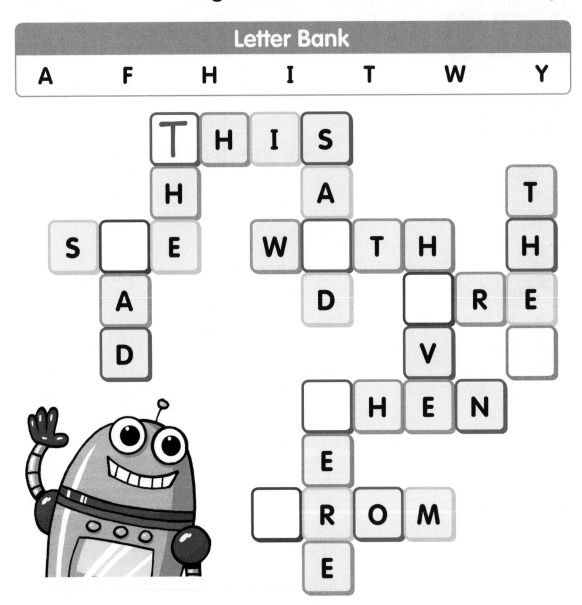

Letter Bank

A	F	H	I	T	W	Y

Write the words from the game board on the lines.

THIS _____ _____ _____

THE _____ _____

_____ _____ _____

Little Skill Seekers

HANDWRITING

Aa

Trace and write.

A A A

a a

Aliyah

ants

Trace and write the sentence.

Aliyah adores ants.

B b

Trace and write.

B B

b b

Bert

bears

Trace and write the sentence.

Bert barks at bears.

C c

Trace and write.

C   C C

c   c c

Cali

cats

Trace and write the sentence.

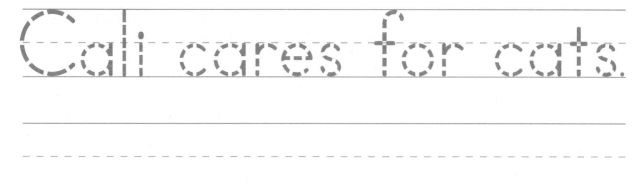

Cali cares for cats.

Dd

Trace and write.

D   D

d   d

Diego

dogs

Trace and write the sentence.

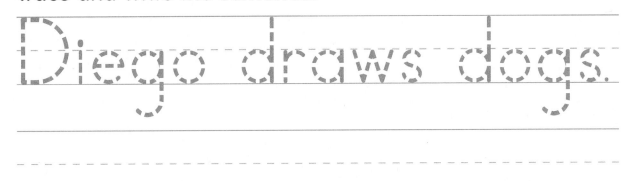

Diego draws dogs.

Ee

Trace and write.

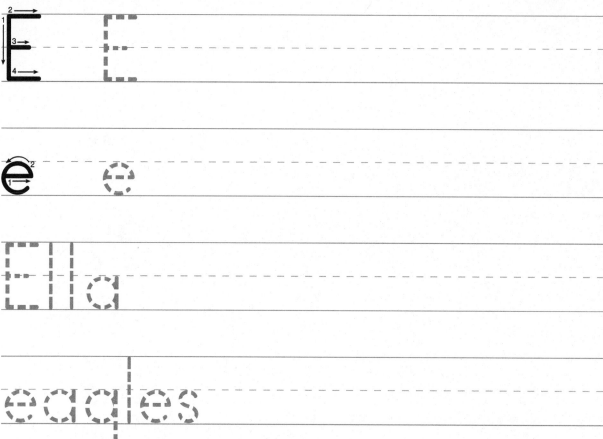

Trace and write the sentence.

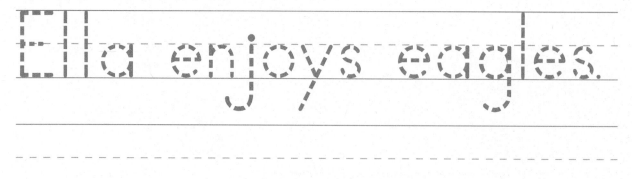

F f

Trace and write.

F   F

f   f

Felix

frogs

Trace and write the sentence.

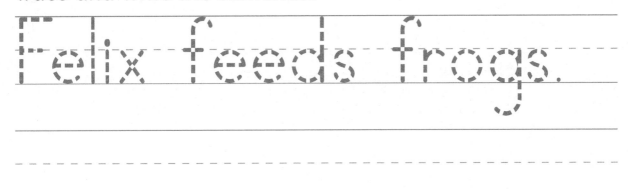

Felix feeds frogs.

Gg

Trace and write.

G G G

g g

Gail

goats

Trace and write the sentence.

Gail grins at goats.

Hh

Trace and write.

H H

h h

Harry

horse

Trace and write the sentence.

Harry has a horse.

I i

Trace and write.

I I

i i

Iris

iguana

Trace and write the sentence.

Iris is an iguana.

Trace and write.

J   J   J

j   j   j

Jamil

jaguars

Trace and write the sentence.

Jamil likes jaguars.

Kk

Trace and write.

K K

k k

Kiara

koala

Trace and write the sentence.

Kiara is a koala.

L l

Trace and write.

L   L

l   l

Logan

lions

Trace and write the sentence.

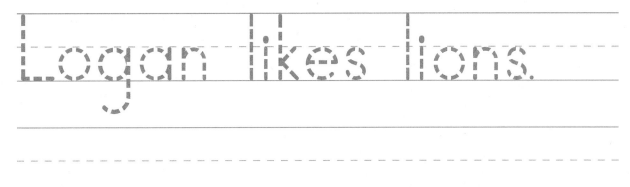

Logan likes lions.

Mm

Trace and write.

M   M

m   m

Mia

monkey

Trace and write the sentence.

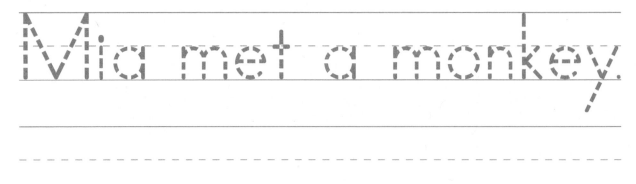

Mia met a monkey.

Nn

Trace and write.

N   N   N

n   n

Neil

newts

Trace and write the sentence.

Neil likes newts.

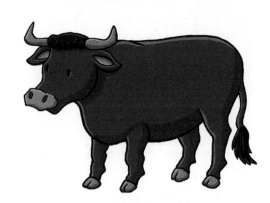

Trace and write.

O O

o o

Olga

oxen

Trace and write the sentence.

Olga owns oxen.

Pp

Trace and write.

P P P

P P

Pablo

parrot

Trace and write the sentence.

Pablo has a parrot.

Qq

Trace and write.

Q   Q

q   q

Quisha

quail

Trace and write the sentence.

Quisha is a quail.

Rr

Trace and write.

R R

r r

Raul

rabbits

Trace and write the sentence.

Raul raises rabbits.

Ss

Trace and write.

S S

s s

Sasha

sheep

Trace and write the sentence.

Sasha sees sheep.

T t

Trace and write.

T T

t t

Tom

tigers

Trace and write the sentence.

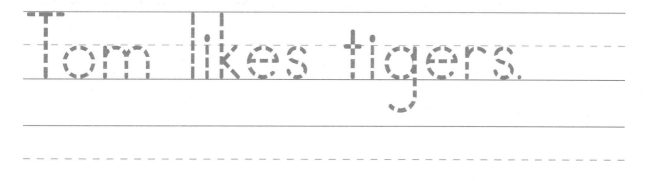

Tom likes tigers.

U u

Trace and write.

U U

u u

Umi

unicorns

Trace and write the sentence.

Umi likes unicorns.

Trace and write.

V V V

V v v

Vito

vulture

Trace and write the sentence.

Vito saw a vulture.

Ww

Trace and write.

whale

Trace and write the sentence.

Wilda saw a whale.

Trace and write.

X X

X X

Xun

x-ray fish

Trace and write the sentence.

Xun is an x-ray fish.

Trace and write.

Y Y Y

y y y

Yara

yaks

Trace and write the sentence.

Yara yaps at yaks.

Zz

Trace and write.

Z Z Z

z z z

Zane

zebra

Trace and write the sentence.

Zane is a zebra.

Numbers 1–10

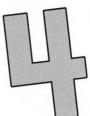

Trace and write.

6 7 8 9 10

Trace and write.

6

7

8

9

10

Color Words

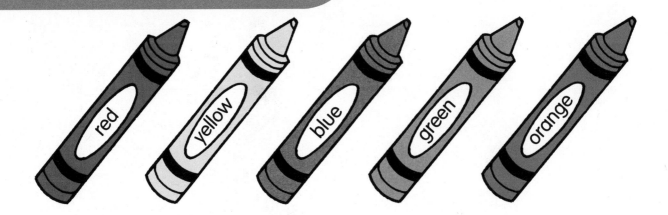

Trace and write.

red

yellow

blue

green

orange

Trace and write.

purple

pink

white

brown

black

Number Words

Trace and write.

one

two

three

four

five

© Scholastic Inc.

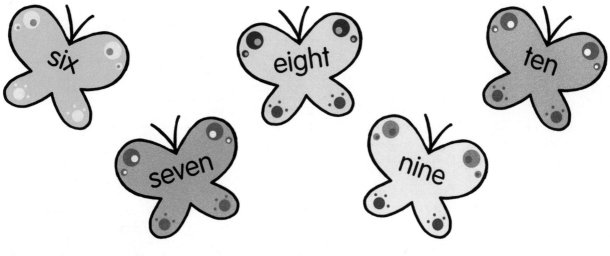

Trace and write.

six

seven

eight

nine

ten

Shapes

Trace and write.

circle

square

triangle

rectangle

oval

Trace and write.

diamond

star

heart

pentagon

octagon

Seasons

Trace and write.

spring

summer

fall

winter

Days of the Week

FRIDAY 22

Trace and write.

Monday

Tuesday

Wednesday

Thursday

Friday

Saturday

Sunday

Months of the Year

Trace and write.

January

February

March

April

May

June

Trace and write.

July

August

September

October

November

December

Farm Animals

Trace and write.

cow

dog

donkey

duck

goose

goat

Trace and write.

hen

horse

pig

rooster

sheep

turkey

Action Words

Trace and write.

cook

eat

walk

drink

read

sleep

Trace and write.

talk

dance

write

run

play

sing

Describing Words

Trace and write.

salty

sweet

sour

spicy

hot

cold

Trace and write.

big

small

tall

pretty

soft

sharp

Describing Words

Trace and write.

loud

hard

dirty

wet

open

closed

© Scholastic Inc.

1 2 3 4

Little Skill Seekers

MATH
SKILLS

Count the flies, bees, and butterflies.
Write how many of each.

Count the corners and sides on each shape.
Write the answers below each shape.

_____ corners

_____ sides

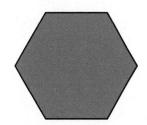

_____ corners

_____ sides

_____ corners

_____ sides

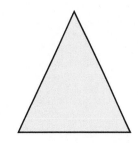

_____ corners

_____ sides

_____ corners

_____ sides

_____ corners

_____ sides

Count. Write your answer. The first one is done for you.

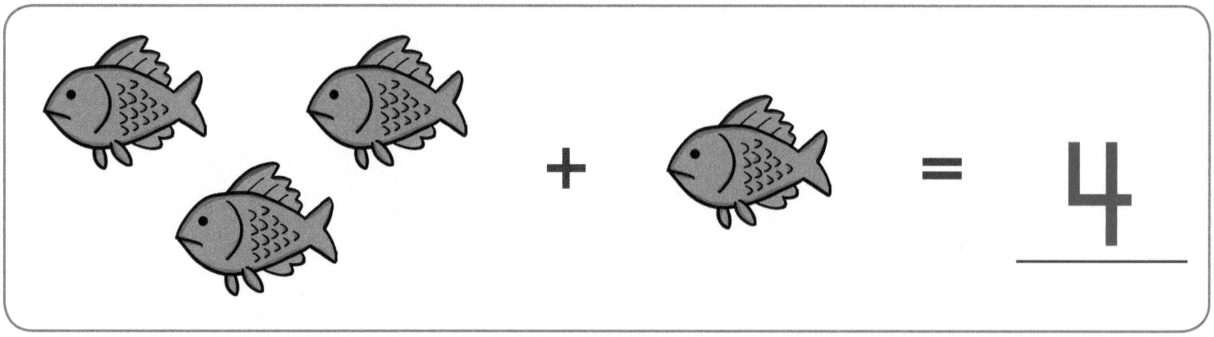

$+$ $=$ **4**

$+$ $=$ _____

$+$ $=$ _____

$+$ $=$ _____

Match each picture to a shape.

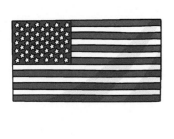 •   •
diamond

 •   •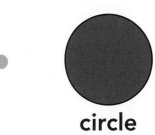
circle

 •   •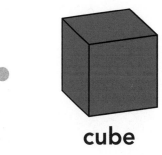
cube

 •   •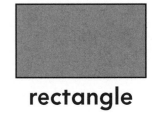
rectangle

 •   •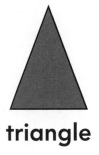
triangle

Count the sets in each pair. Write the number.
Then, circle the set that has fewer.

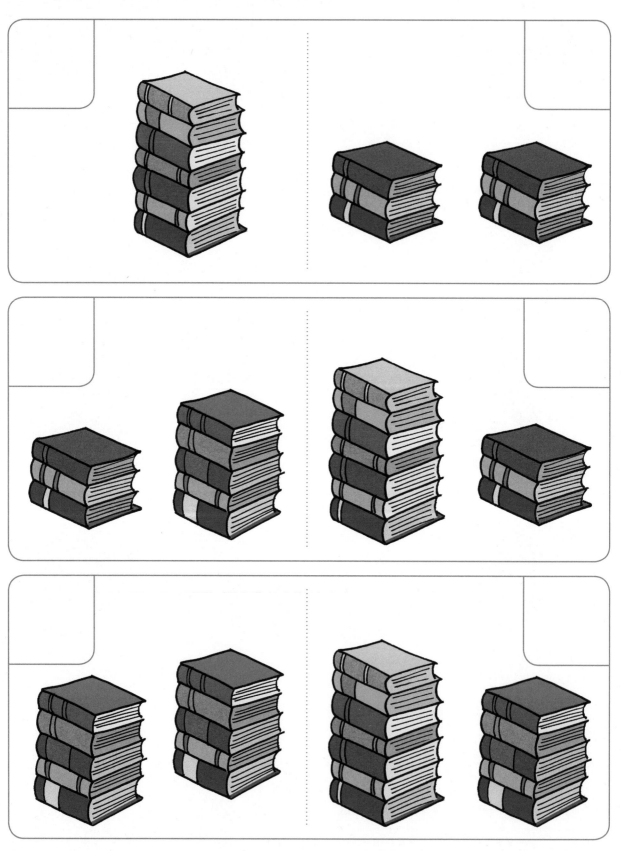

Color each shape that is divided into equal halves.

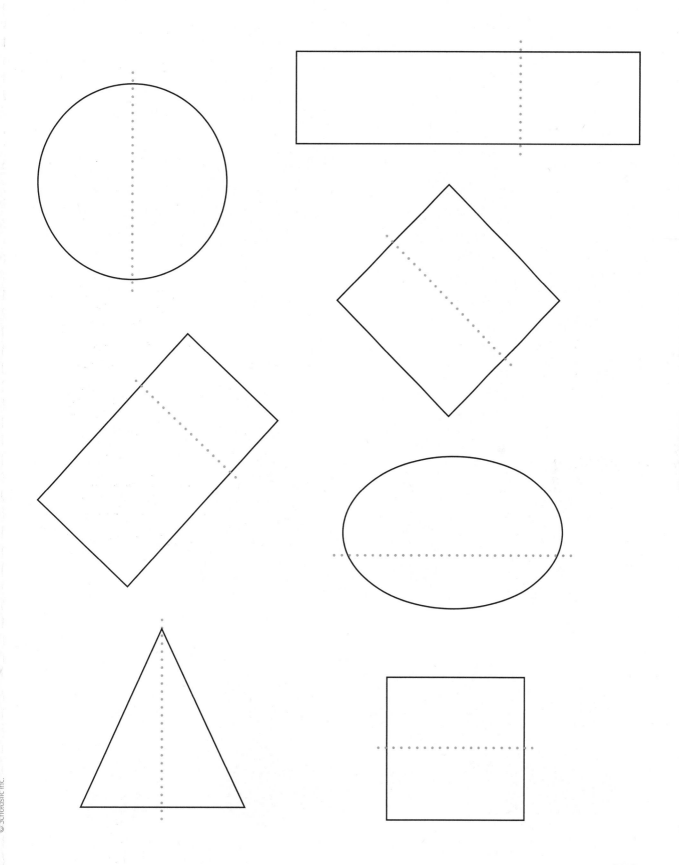

Count. Write your answer.

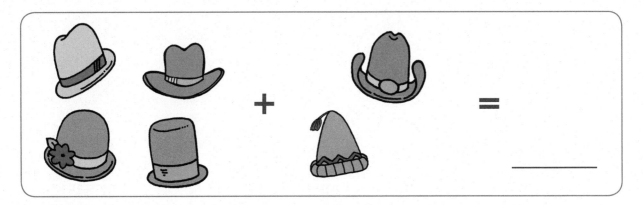

Count. How many are left when some are taken away? Draw it. Then, write the numbers below the pictures.

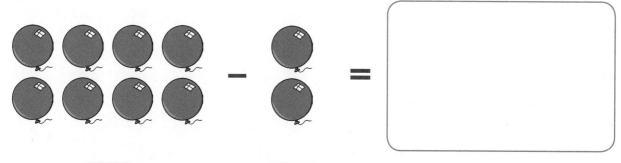

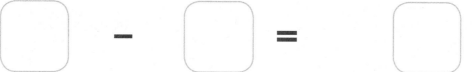

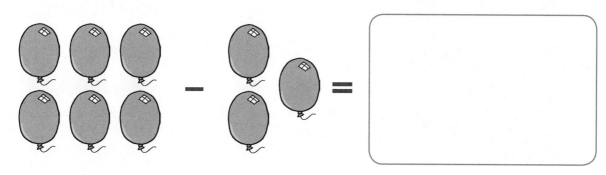

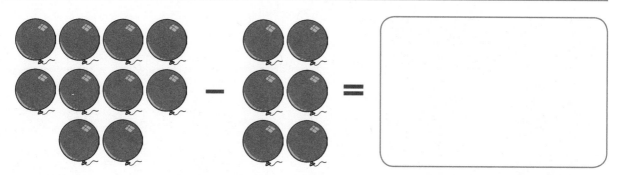

Match the groups with the same number of crayons.

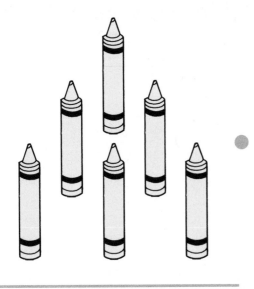

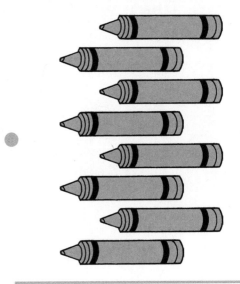

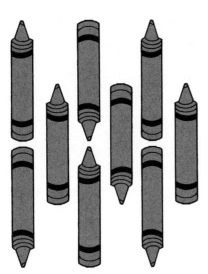

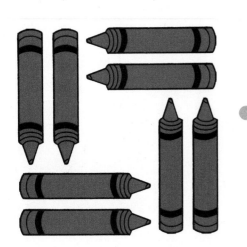

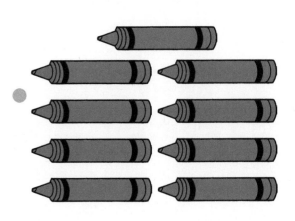

What comes next? Draw it.

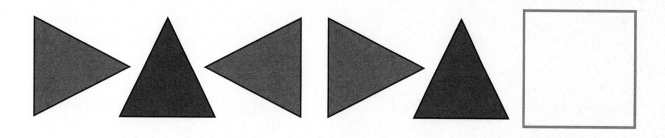

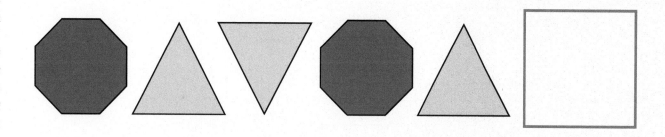

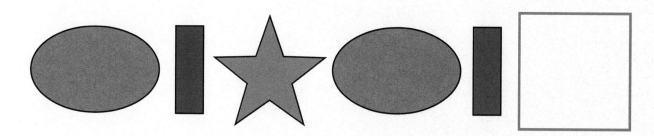

Count. Write the number. Add.

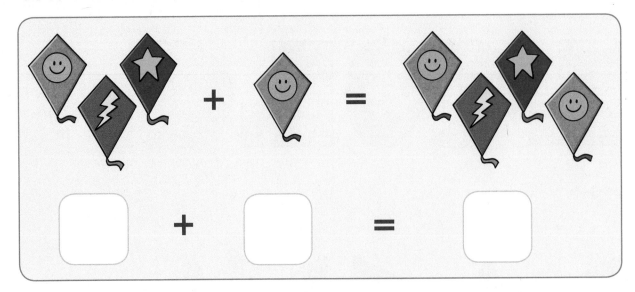

$$\boxed{} + \boxed{} = \boxed{}$$

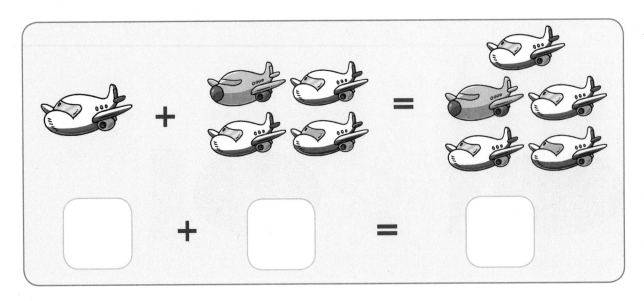

Count the animals in each set. Write the number.

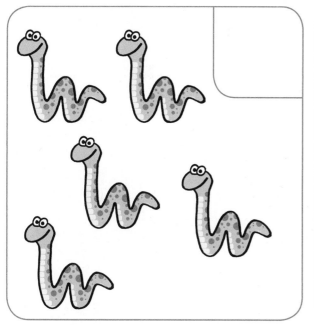

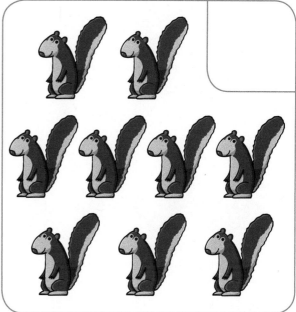

How many owls and snakes in all?

  +  **=**

Match each picture to a shape.

 •

•

square

 •

•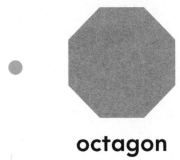

octagon

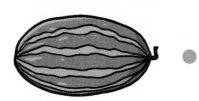 •

•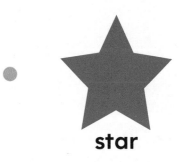

star

 •

•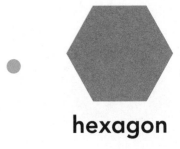

hexagon

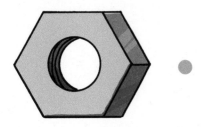 •

•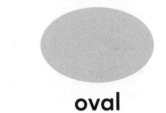

oval

Count. How many are left when some are taken away? Draw it. Then, write the numbers below the pictures.

$$\boxed{} - \boxed{} = \boxed{}$$

$$\boxed{} - \boxed{} = \boxed{}$$

$$\boxed{} - \boxed{} = \boxed{}$$

Count the fish. Write how many of each.

Count. Write the number. Add.

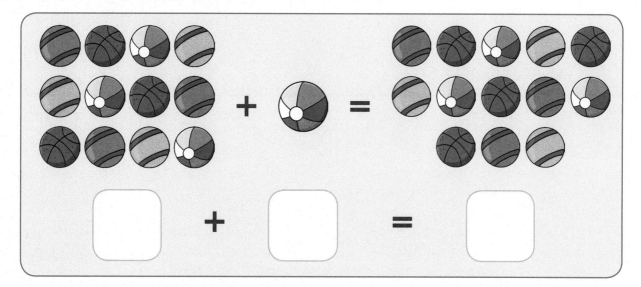

Draw the missing shape.

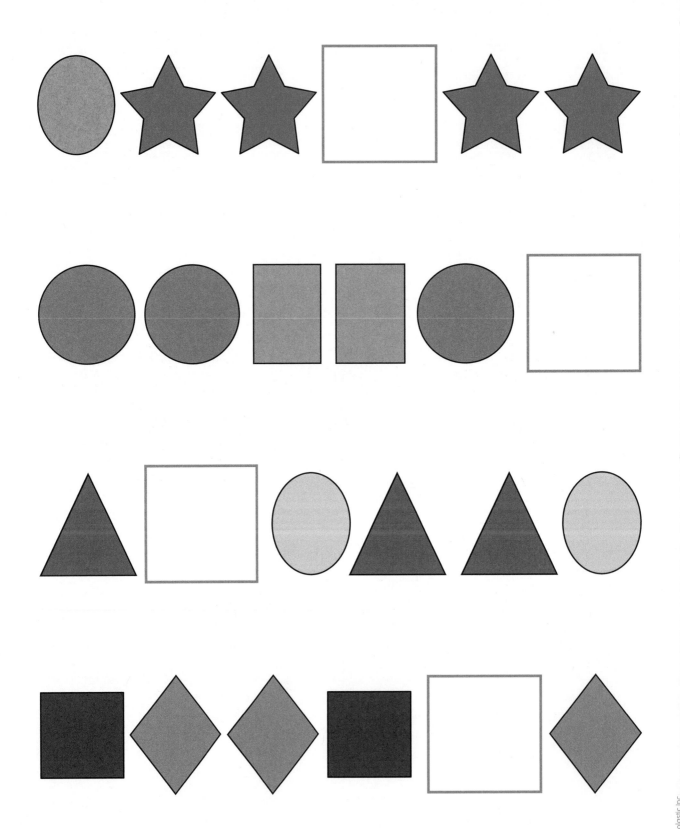

Compare the pictures in each row.
Write 1, 2, and 3 to order the pictures by size.

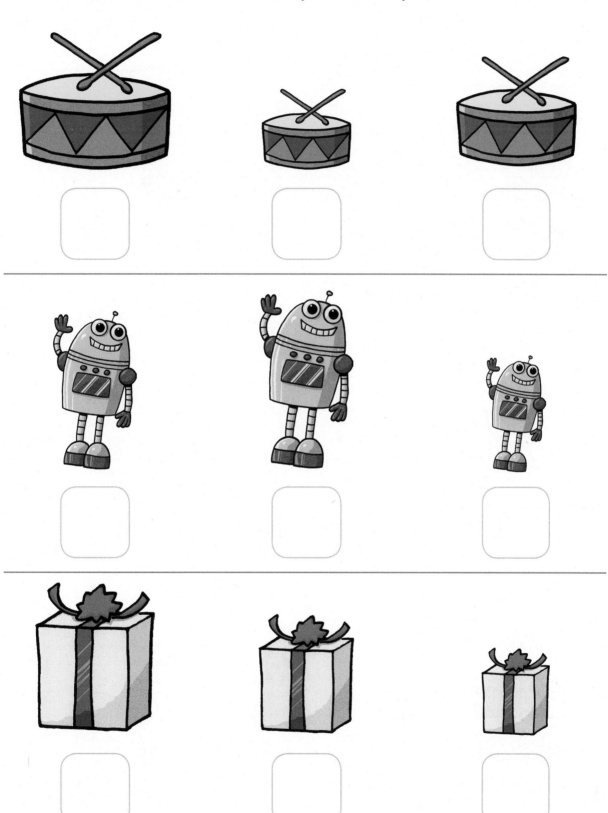

© Scholastic Inc.

Count the sets in each in each pair. Write the number. Then, circle the set that has more.

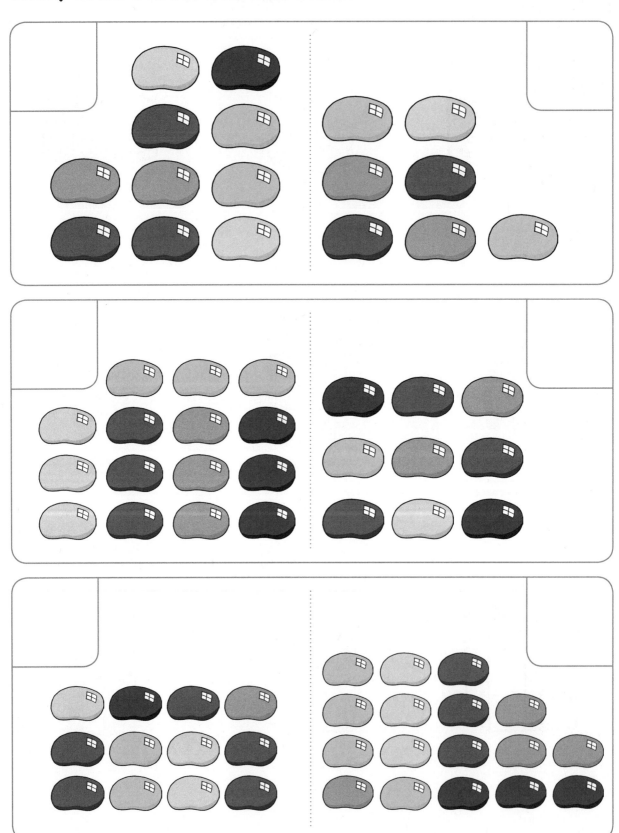

Count. How many are left when some are taken away? Draw it. Then, write the numbers below the pictures.

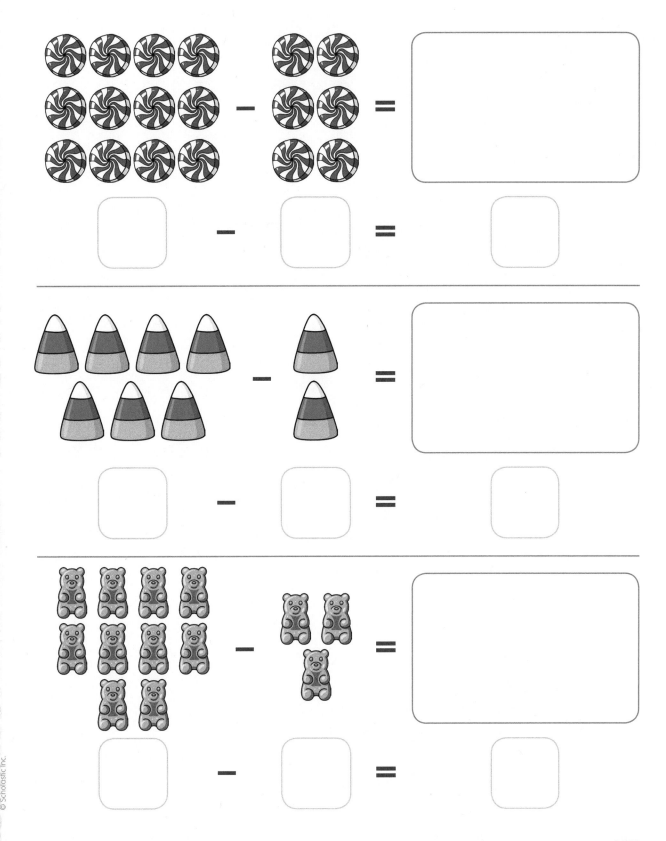

Draw the missing shape.

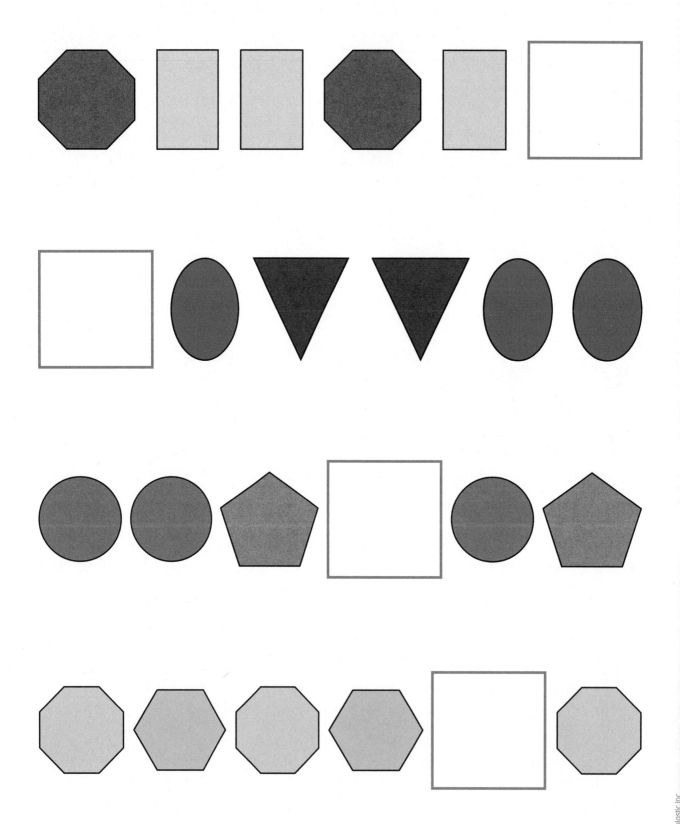

Count the bugs in each set. Write the number.

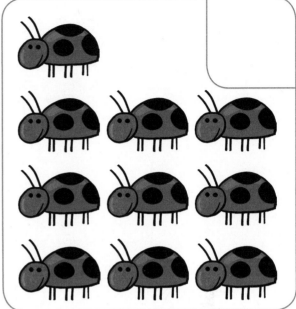

How many ladybugs and spiders in all?

 ___ **+** ___ **=** ___

Count. Write the number. Add.

$$\square \quad + \quad \square \quad = \quad \square$$

$$\square \quad + \quad \square \quad = \quad \square$$

$$\square \quad + \quad \square \quad = \quad \square$$

Draw the other half of each shape.

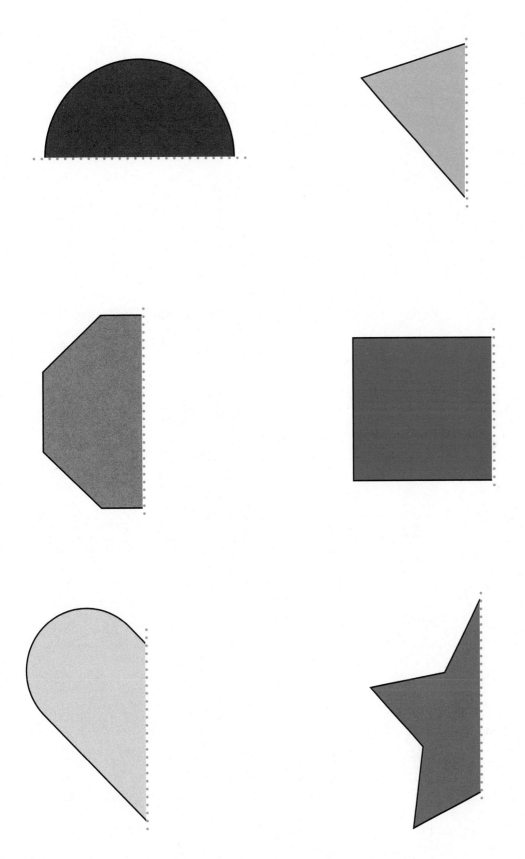

Match the groups with the same number of cupcakes.

Draw a marble in each empty space to make 20.
Write the number you drew to finish each number sentence.

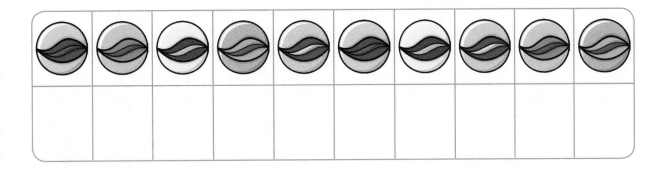

$$10 + \underline{\quad} = 20$$

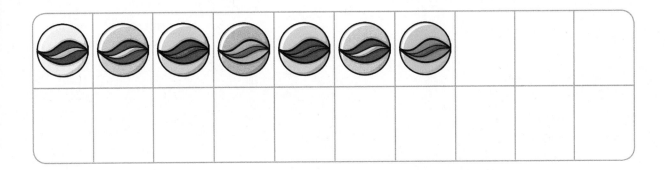

$$7 + \underline{\quad} = 20$$

$$15 + \underline{\quad} = 20$$

Answer Key For pages not shown, please check your child's work.

Choose a word from the list to complete the sentences.

Sight Words

a	as	I	in	is	it	on	to

1. This **is** my sister Molly.

2. I have **a** brother too. His name is Paul.

3. Paul and **I** like to swim.

4. Today is as sunny **as** yesterday.

5. **It** is a good day for the beach.

6. We go **to** the beach on sunny days.

7. Molly, what is **in** your beach bag?

8. Paul, put **on** your swim suit.

REMEMBER TO capitalize the first word in a sentence.

83

Choose a word from the list to complete the sentences.

Sight Words

an	at	be	by	he	of	or	we

1. I have a twin brother. **We** are in the first grade.

2. We go to school **by** bus.

3. Mom always says, "Don't **be** late."

4. The bus comes **at** 8:00 A.M.

5. We must leave early **or** we will miss it.

6. This is a picture **of** George.

7. **He** is the school bus driver.

8. George does **an** important job.

REMEMBER TO capitalize the first word in a sentence.

91

Choose a word from the list to complete the sentences.

Sight Words

all	and	are	but	can	for	had	the

1. My sisters are **all** older.

2. Lina is 11, Jenna is 13, **and** Ria is 15.

3. Ria is older, **but** Jenna is taller.

4. Jenna and Lina **are** in middle school.

5. They take **the** bus to school.

6. Lina ran **for** class president.

7. She **had** the most votes.

8. I **can** be class president too one day.

99

Choose a word from the list to complete the sentences.

Sight Words

from	not	one	they	this	want	with	you

1. Maya's family is **from** Utah.

2. **They** moved here last year.

3. **This** is their house.

4. Maya's Grandma lives **with** them.

5. Maya is **one** of my best friends.

6. Maya and I **want** to travel.

7. We do **not** know where yet.

8. **You** can come too!

REMEMBER TO capitalize the first word in a sentence.

107

Choose a word from the list to complete the sentences.

Sight Words

have	said	she	that	was	were	when	your

1. Yesterday **was** the first day of school.

2. Ms. Pat will be our new teacher.

   She teaches first grade.

3. She **said** she loves teaching.

4. What is **your** name?

5. **When** did you start school?

6. **Were** you in Kindergarten last year?

7. We will **have** a holiday party this year.

8. I know **that** you will love our class.

REMEMBER TO capitalize the first word in a sentence.

CLASSROOM JOBS

115

Complete the sentences. Choose a word from the list. Write the words in the puzzle. The first one is done for you.

Sight Words

that
the
they
was
what
with

Across

2. Where are **they** going?

3. I walk to school **with** friends.

4. He **was** at camp all summer.

Down

1. Where is **the** dog?

2. Is **that** a new car?

3. **What** is your name?

REMEMBER TO capitalize the first word in a sentence.

116

Some words on the board are missing letters. Use the Letter Bank. Fill in the missing letters. The first one is done for you.

Letter Bank

A	F	H	I	T	W	Y

Write the words from the game board on the lines.

THIS HAD HAVE WHEN
THE SAID ARE WERE
SHE WITH THEY FROM

118

192

© Scholastic Inc.